SPIN

Tips and tactics to win at table tennis

Tom Lodziak

ISBN: 9798666492536

For Jodi, Franz, Beatrix and Oliver
for supporting my table tennis obsession

Contents

Amateur table tennis

It's a wet December evening in 2019. I'm on my way to play a match in the Cambridge Table Tennis League. This is an amateur league, but the standard is decent. I'm the designated driver. I pick up my teammates and attempt to chat, follow the instructions on my sat nav and drive in the dark, all at the same time. Inevitably, I take a wrong turning which adds an extra few minutes to the journey. This is fairly typical of my driving. I have yet to master the skill of talking and driving simultaneously.

Eventually, we arrive at the venue. We are playing in the canteen of a secondary school. The floor is a little slippery. The lighting is a little dark. Chairs and tables are stacked up in the middle of the canteen. If the ball lands in this area, it can be a mission to get the ball back. The team we are playing only has two players. The third player dropped out with illness. Welcome to the world of amateur table tennis!

This is the top division. I have never beaten my two opponents before. My record against both players is: played four, lost four. But tonight I am quietly confident. I am playing well this season. My results have improved. I daydream about winning both matches. This makes me happy. My first match is against Geoff - a player 20 years older than me. What he lacks in physical athleticism, he makes up with tactical mastery. In the first two games he gives me a table tennis lesson. He exposes my weaknesses and forces me to play at his tempo. Geoff controls the game, pulling me out very wide on my forehand and then punishing me wide to my backhand. He leads 11-4, 11-6. I make a fleeting comeback in the third game, but this is more due to Geoff temporarily switching off, rather than anything significant that I do. I win this game 11-5. Geoff refocuses for the 4th game and once again uses all his tactical experience to out-think and out-play me. He wins the match comfortably. We shake hands, exchange a couple of pleasantries and I sink into my chair. It's not a great start to my evening. I feel very frustrated that I was unable to play better. I don't mind losing, but it does annoy me if I don't play well. In this match I didn't play well.

Half an hour passes and it is my turn to play again. I am a bit more fired up now. I have stopped caring if I win or lose. I just want to play well. My opponent is Jan - a tall and friendly German player. He likes to go back from the table and play with very heavy topspin. This suits me. It allows me to use my blocks and counter-attacks. Last time we played it was close. I decide to start aggressively and give Jan something to worry about. The game plan works. I hit lots of attacking shots. Jan is a little off the pace. He struggles to return my attacks. I win the first game 11-5.

The second game is closer. Jan's level improves. He makes it harder for me to attack. I push more which allows Jan to attack first with his heavy topspin loops. As the game progresses, we both try to be the aggressor. We both have successes. We both make mistakes. We are evenly matched. The score is 10-10. I need to take some risks. It's Jan's serve. I decide to flick rather than push. This surprises Jan. He plays a weak shot to the middle of the table. I step to the left and attack very aggressively with my forehand. The ball lands right in the corner of the table. Jan can't get to the ball. My point. I now have a game point, but I'm not too focused on the score. I'm playing well and want to keep being aggressive. I pause for a moment and visualise the serve and third ball attack I want to do. I choose a backhand serve with sidespin and topspin. I know the ball is likely to be returned with topspin. I am prepared for this. I serve. Jan struggles to control the spin. His return is a little too high. I once again hit the ball hard with my forehand, this time to the other corner. Boom! Jan can't return the ball. I win the game 12-10.

I am now leading 2-0 against a player I have not beaten before. As we change ends I make a psychological error. I start thinking about the result. I'm winning 2-0. I think I can win this, but what if I mess up? What if Jan makes a comeback? OK, I'm not actually sure I can do this. My mind has lost focus. I start to feel a bit of pressure. My anxiety levels increase. Inevitably, I play poorly in the third game. I am tight and too tentative. I make a few unforced errors. I stop attacking. Jan starts to dominate. He loops with heavy topspin and if I do return these attacks, he powers the next ball past me. Jan wins the game 11-3.

The tide has turned. I started the match strongly, but Jan came back in the second game and easily won the third game. There is a real danger Jan will complete a comeback and win the match. I need to sort out my head. I try hard to refocus. I need to start attacking again. This is how I won the first two games. I don't want to get bogged down with backspin and pushing. I decide to turn it into a topspin match. I serve mostly topspin. I try to return most serves with flicks and loops, but my game plan isn't working. I make a few unforced attacking errors. The score is 7-4 to Jan. I can feel the match slipping away from me.

I try to compose myself and relax my body. Breathe. Take your time. I decide to keep on attacking. I may as well lose trying to go for my shots, rather than retreating into a passive shell. Jan serves. I flick to Jan's body.

look equally naff in our sweaty t-shirts, baggy shorts or tracksuit bottoms. No one cares about your background, whether you're a millionaire or have no job at all. All that matters in the table tennis hall is table tennis.

This army of amateur players just love to play. Most of us don't aspire to be a professional player and become world champion. We have more modest goals. We just want to improve. We want to beat a friend, family member, work colleague, club-mate or arch-nemesis. We want to improve our win percentage. We want to move up a division. We want to progress further in a tournament. We just want to get better at this weirdly addictive game.

This is the reason I have written this book. It is a book to help amateur table tennis players improve their skills, win more points and win more matches. I have been playing table tennis obsessively for the past 13 years. During this time I have been coached and gained valuable insight from a number of top players and coaches, including Richard Prause (Timo Boll's former coach), Rade Markovic, Desmond Douglas, Matthew Syed, Craig Bryant, Mark Mitchell, Ferenc Horvath and Eli Baraty.

I've played hundreds of local league games, winning far more than I have lost. I have written over 200 articles about table tennis on my website. I have made over 100 video tutorials for my YouTube channel. I have coached hundreds of players - beginner, intermediate and advanced. I have a wealth of table tennis tips which I want to share with you. Tips on training, service, returning serves, winning points, tactics, playing matches and continual improvement. These are tips which work at amateur level. Tips which are achievable. Tips which will make a difference, even if you only play one hour per week.

I make no apology. I'm not a great table tennis player. I have never played professionally. I have never won a tournament of any significance. I am just a decent amateur player, who has progressed from the bottom division of a local league to the top division. But maybe my experience will resonate with you. My struggles are very likely to be similar to your struggles. The strategies I have used to progress in amateur table tennis are very likely to work for you too. I may not be a world champion, but I have a way of playing and teaching table tennis which will hopefully be very relevant to you.

Some of my advice may seem counter to the general consensus. But all the advice I share is based upon what I have actually experienced playing amateur table tennis. What works in amateur table tennis may not work at the professional level. But if you don't play at the professional level - and don't aspire to - then it doesn't really matter. You may not always agree with what I say - that's fine - but at least give consideration to my ideas. The tips I share have worked for me or other players I know. If these tips work for me - with my funny technique, dodgy knees and the coordination of a giraffe wearing ice skates - then they can definitely work for you too!

One quick note - throughout the book I switch between 'he', 'him, 'she' and 'her' when referring to a non-specific player. This is not say that each example only applies to either a male or female. I have just tried to simplify the prose. Please use your imagination to substitute the preferred gender pronoun where relevant.

Before we get into the details of improving and winning more points, I want to tell you a bit more about my table tennis background. This will help put this book into context. Are you ready? Let's play!

My table tennis story

Let's rewind to 2004. I was competing in my first tournament. The British Universities & Colleges Sport (BUCS) Table Tennis Championships. This was a tournament for the best university table tennis players studying in the UK. I was representing Southampton University.

I thought I was pretty good at table tennis, but during the tournament I was going to learn how utterly terrible I really was. One of my teammates, who had played in the tournament before, said I'd do OK. She was either being very kind, or was massively overestimating how good I was. But I was reassured. Maybe I would do OK. I was excited.

This excitement didn't last long. I walked into the tournament hall and my mouth dropped. Everyone knocking up looked amazingly good at table tennis. They were looping the ball back and forth, metres back from the table, playing shots I'd never seen before. I couldn't even topspin a ball. I found a quiet corner and hid away until it was my turn to play. I opened my bag and inspected my trusty £5 table tennis bat. This was the bat I had used on family holidays as a child. The rubbers were dead. A plaster on the handle covered up a protruding nail. But I liked it. It was familiar. It gave me some comfort as I prepared to take on these seriously intimidating table tennis players.

I played my first group match. Guess what happened? I got slaughtered. I barely won a point. The other player was just smashing balls past me. I spent more time picking the ball up from the floor than actually playing table tennis. Next match, I got thrashed again. This time to a Harry Potter look-alike. And he certainly did have some wizardly table tennis skills. He was a defender and was spinning the ball in ways I just couldn't fathom. No balls were smashed past me in this match. Instead, I made all the mistakes. Balls in the net. Balls off the end of the table. I just couldn't get any kind of rally going. This defeat felt somehow worse, as my opponent exposed how completely clueless I was. Again, I barely won a point.

By my third group match, I was already desperate to go home. I had been thrashed twice and knew what was coming in the third match. Yes, another massive beating. This time I was facing some sort of service demon. Unbelievable serves. So much spin. I had no idea what to do. My attempted returns were spraying everywhere - the net, the sky, the floor. I don't recall returning a single serve.

Three matches. Three losses. Hardly any points won. I felt embarrassed for the players I was losing to, as they were so much better than me. I was humiliated. I really wasn't very good at table tennis. I stopped playing for two years after this, as I was clearly rubbish.

The beginning

My first memory of playing table tennis was far more enjoyable. I was aged 7. It was summer and I was on a campsite somewhere in France. Twenty children from different countries were running around a table, trying to hit the ball over the net.

the ball before I do? I had no way to stop these players smashing the ball past me. I was helpless. Humiliated.

The players I lost to in the group stage didn't survive long in the tournament either. They were soundly beaten by even better players. I was a thousand levels behind the two players who made the final. So I gave up. The mountain was far too high to climb.

Starting again

Two and a half years passed. Then another family holiday. This time to a more exotic destination - Sri Lanka. My eldest brother, Stephen, was getting married. Off we flew - me, all the family, and my girlfriend Jodi. Like all good holiday resorts, our hotel had a table tennis table. I am one of four brothers. It didn't take long for the competitive urges to return. We all like to beat each other at whatever we do - card games, quizzes, music competitions, running races, arm wrestles, and of course, table tennis. At the hotel, the table was located inside in a small and very hot room. The net was flimsy and the table was a bit unstable, but we didn't mind. We took it in turns to play. Once again I remembered how much I enjoyed playing, especially when the competition was a bit easier. I may be useless compared to the best university players, but I was now champion of the Lodziak brothers!

I vowed to start playing table tennis again when I returned home, which was now North London. And that's what I did. I found a club - Finsbury Table Tennis Club - which was quite close to where I worked. The coach, Sanket, was very welcoming. The club had a range of abilities. Some very good players attended, but also many who were very average, like me. I fitted in and played every week. I trained hard and played against all kinds of weird and wonderful styles. I was 27-years-old and this was the first time in my life I had played table tennis regularly.

It was only a matter of time before the inevitable happened. The coach Sanket asked me if I wanted to join a league team. Of course, I was flattered and said yes. The coach must think I'm decent and have potential. In hindsight, this was a little wide of the mark. I've been in the table tennis scene for so long now, I know the real truth. *Anyone* who shows a tiny bit of enthusiasm for table tennis will be asked to join a team at some point. Clubs are always desperate for players. You don't have to be a special talent with hidden potential. Anyone will do to make up the numbers! But I was in the team. I was going to play competitive table tennis again.

After a year of training and gradual improvement, I was ready. I had even learnt how to topspin the ball a little. I felt confident that I could win plenty of matches. I wasn't going to be humiliated like I was at the university tournament. It was time for my first competitive league match in the bottom division of the Central London Table Tennis League. I knew I was playing better than ever, certainly a lot better than when I was at university. I had high hopes, but as my first league match approached, something odd happened. I felt really anxious. My mouth was dry. My legs were heavy. My heart rate was in overdrive. I could feel the eyes of everyone in the room looking at me. I wanted to be somewhere else, anywhere else, other than in this table tennis hall. I was a nervous wreck!

Guess what? I lost all three matches. But there was a glimmer of hope. I wasn't outclassed. The matches were competitive. I even took one opponent to five games. Even though I was very nervous before the league match started, I felt OK afterwards. In fact, I felt hungry for more.

I wasn't that far away from beating these players. With a bit more training, a bit more experience, I could win.

Table tennis addiction

This is when my table tennis addiction really started. I increased the number of hours I trained each week. I read table tennis books. I watched table tennis videos. I trained with more of a purpose. I eagerly soaked up any tips from more experienced players and the club coach Sanket. I even attended a week-long table tennis residential course in Durham, where I got to hang out with Matthew Syed - one of the best English players over the past 30 years. I purchased a proper table tennis bat. I even wore a proper table tennis shirt. I was taking table tennis more seriously.

My results gradually improved over the five years I played in London. I moved up a division. This was tough. There were no easy matches. Every opponent was that bit more consistent. They had better serves. They could generate more spin. But despite the losses in the higher division, I was still competitive. These players weren't *that much* better than me. If I could make small improvements to my game, I could beat some of these players. More training. More experimentation with technique and tactics. More observation of better players. More money spent on new rubbers and blades! In the higher division I ended up just about winning as many matches as I lost, but it took a lot of effort to get there.

With help from Sanket, I set up a new club - Highbury Table Tennis Club. I also studied for my first coaching qualification. I was getting even more involved in table tennis. Table tennis was becoming a central part of my identity. I would play imaginary table tennis shots when walking down the street. I would have debates about table tennis tactics with myself. I would have dreams about table tennis, usually after a poor performance. I now had a serious table tennis obsession.

Coaching in Cambridge

My first child, Franz, was born in 2011. Jodi, Franz and I lived in a one-bedroom flat, opposite Clissold Park in North London. A small baby takes up a surprising amount of space, and we soon outgrew the flat. We tried to find a bigger property to buy in London, but the prices were far too crazy for us to afford anything near where we lived. We kept looking further and further in the outskirts of London, but still no joy. Eventually, in 2013, we decided to move to Cambridge, the city where I grew up. A new start for both our small little family and also my table tennis.

I found a job doing digital marketing for an education company. But in the evenings and weekends - and sometimes lunch breaks too! - I would do 1-to-1 table tennis coaching. Students, city workers, kids, 80-year-olds - I would coach anyone who showed an interest in table tennis. I found I had an ability to teach table tennis in a way that resonated with the players who came to see me. I've never been a top player, never represented my country, never played professionally. I am a decent amateur player, and I could really understand and empathise with the struggles of the amateur players I coached. They were my struggles too.

Over the next five years, I coached more and more players. Eventually, I reached a tipping point. It became financially viable for me to coach table tennis as a full-time career. I did procrastinate about this

Training

The training hall is where we spend a lot of time hitting balls, doing drills, playing practice matches and having fun. It's where we try to develop our game - try to get better at table tennis. But how we train makes a big difference to how much we improve. Some players like to spend a lot of time hitting forehand to forehand and backhand to backhand. Some players devise complex drills, to test their skills to the limit. Some players like to skip the drills and just play lots of matches. Some players turn up, have a chat, and just do some random, unstructured play. Some players never bother to train at all!

What is the best - the smartest - way to train? Should we drill, drill, drill until our bodies are sore? Should we freestyle with lots of random play? Should we play lots of matches? How can we use whatever training time we have available to maximise our improvement? These are some questions I shall explore in this chapter. First, let's look at how long it takes to get really good at table tennis. The answer may surprise you.

How long does it take to get really good at table tennis?

Table tennis is a tough sport. I have coached many beginners and improvers who are surprised by just how much there is to learn and how difficult table tennis is to master. Maybe there is a general perception that table tennis is an easy game. Almost everyone at some point has played some form of ping pong. And they have probably been able to hit the ball over the net - "See, that wasn't very difficult".

However, to play competitive table tennis to a high standard is a different matter. Table tennis is a very complex sport, with lots of different shots, spins and playing styles, played at a frighteningly fast pace. There is a lot to learn and master. It does take time to get really good at table tennis, but how long? Can you become a really good table tennis player quickly or will it take years and years? And what's the best way to improve quickly? Let's explore these questions.

What is a "really good" player?

Firstly, what do I mean by a "really good" player? This is a tough question, as there are so many levels.

A bottom division local league player will be considered "really good" compared to a social player who has never played competitively, but wouldn't be considered "really good" compared to a middle division local league player.

A middle division local league player will be considered "really good" compared to a bottom division player, but wouldn't be considered "really good" compared to a top division local league player.

A top division local league player will be considered "really good" compared to a middle division local league player, but wouldn't be considered "really good" compared to a player ranked in the top 100 in England.

A player ranked in the top 100 in England will be considered "really good" compared to almost all players in the rest of the country, but wouldn't be considered "really good" compared to a player ranked in the top 5 in England.

A player in the top 5 in England is likely to be a professional player. To most people, these players are absolutely amazing, but they are likely to get beaten consistently by players in the top 20 in the world. A player in the top 20 in the world is *unbelievable* at table tennis, but may get easily beaten by the best player in the world - the player sitting at the top of the global rankings.

There is always a higher standard. There is always a better player, unless you are number one in the world. However, it's not helpful to use the world's number one player as a benchmark. It's not really that helpful to use professional players as a benchmark for "really good" either. This standard is unreachable for most of us.

For the purposes of this book, let's say a Division 1 local league player – ranked somewhere in the top 500 in England – is a "really good" table tennis player. This is a standard most players in local league aspire to reach, and it is attainable. You don't have to be a full-time athlete to reach this standard. You can play table tennis in your spare time and be a top division player. For U.S. readers of my book, I guess the equivalent is a 2000 rating. I appreciate this is a subjective definition, but it's better to have some sort of definition to work with than none at all.

The long learning process

From my experience, it can take 5-15 years of dedicated practice to reach a "really good" standard. Yes, this is quite a wide time frame, but so much depends on how much a player practises. A player who practises a lot, may be nearer to the 5-year end of the time frame. A player who practises less frequently may be more towards the 15-year end of the time frame. It can be done quicker than 5-15 years (more on this later). And for many players it can take even longer – a lifetime of playing, and they still might not be able to get there.

This time frame is not based on any data, although it would be fascinating to see a proper study of how long it takes players to reach a Division 1 local league standard. This time frame is based purely on my observations of seeing players improve in local league table tennis over the past decade. In short, it can take a very long time to get really good at playing table tennis.

It takes a long time to master table tennis as there is just so much to learn. Let's start with the strokes. You need to be able to consistently play a lot of different attacking and defensive strokes. This includes:

Attacking strokes

- Forehand drive
- Backhand drive

- Forehand topspin vs backspin
- Backhand topspin vs backspin
- Forehand topspin vs block
- Backhand topspin vs block
- Forehand flick
- Backhand flick
- Forehand counter drive/topspin
- Backhand counter drive/topspin
- Forehand counter loop
- Forehand smash

Defensive strokes

- Forehand push
- Backhand push
- Forehand block
- Backhand block
- Forehand lob
- Backhand lob
- Forehand chop
- Backhand chop

But just playing single strokes isn't enough. You also have to master the transition from one stroke to another stroke.

Transitions

- Push > block
- Push > topspin
- Topspin vs backspin > topspin vs block
- Block > topspin
- Flick > topspin
- Lob > counter loop
- Topspin > smash

But the ball doesn't always go to the same position. You have to master switching from forehand to backhand and backhand to forehand for all the above strokes.

Switching

- Forehand stroke > Backhand stroke
- Backhand stroke > Forehand stroke

But you can't always play your strokes in exactly the same way. You need to adjust your strokes depending on how much spin is on the ball.

Stroke adjustments

- Adjusting strokes for heavy backspin
- Adjusting strokes for light backspin

- Adjusting strokes for heavy topspin
- Adjusting strokes for light topspin
- Adjusting strokes for no spin

Your game is certainly coming along now, but to reach a higher level, you need to be able to play all of your strokes to different positions on the table.

Shot placement

- Forehand down the line
- Forehand cross-court
- Forehand to middle
- Backhand down the line
- Backhand cross-court
- Backhand to middle

Having good strokes, being able to switch between different strokes, making stroke adjustments and being able to place the ball to different positions is no good, if your footwork sucks. You also need to have good footwork.

Footwork

- Side to side footwork
- In and out footwork

- Close to table > mid-distance footwork
- Forehand pivot footwork
- Crossover footwork

Now you have good strokes, can transition between strokes, can adjust your strokes for different amounts of spin, can place your shots to different positions and can move well. But you're never going to be any good unless you have decent serves.

Service

- Backspin serve
- Sidespin serve
- Topspin serve
- No spin serve
- Service tactics
- Service variations

But serves on their own are no good. When you play advanced players, most of your serves will be returned. You also need to learn how to follow up your serves.

- 3rd ball attack
- 5th ball attack
- 7th ball attack

Your service game is only 50% of points. This won't be enough to win matches. You also need to know how to return serves.

Returning serves

- Reading service spin
- Returning backspin serves
- Returning sidespin serves
- Returning topspin serves
- Returning no spin serves

To make it even harder, you need to know how to play against different playing styles. You need a book's worth of match tactics stored in your brain, ready to use against every weird and wonderful playing style. What works against one opponent may not work against another. You have to choose the best tactics to use against each opponent you play.

Match tactics

- Tactics for playing a pusher
- Tactics for playing a chopper
- Tactics for playing a blocker
- Tactics for playing a lobber
- Tactics for playing a topspin attacker
- Tactics for playing a mid-distance looper

- Tactics for playing a flat hitter
- Tactics for playing a one wing attacker
- Tactics for playing a long pimples player
- Tactics for playing a short pimples player
- Tactics for playing an anti-spin player

Having a good tactical game is no good if you freeze whenever you play a competitive match. You also have to deal with the psychological aspect of competing.

Mindset

- Dealing with pressure
- Controlling your nerves
- Staying focused
- Playing without tension
- Keeping a clear head

Muscle memory

As you can see from the list above, there is a huge amount you have to master. I have listed 74 things you need to do well to be a "really good" table tennis player. I'm sure there are many other things I have missed. The list is undoubtedly even longer. If the list above isn't daunting enough, it gets harder still. All the above needs to be learned to the level where it is stored in your subconscious.

took me 10 years to progress from the bottom division of a local league to the top division. 10 years!

Table tennis is a difficult game. It takes most people a long time to master. You shouldn't get despondent if your progress is slow. One of the great things about table tennis is that you can play the sport your entire life. To play at a "really good" level, you don't have to be a young 20-something-year-old. You can be in your sixties and seventies and still be able to compete at a high local league level.

Take your time. Don't rush. The longer you play table tennis and the more you practise, the more you will improve. Improvement doesn't always happen in a straight line. There are ups and downs. But if you practise with a purpose, your general progress should be an upwards trajectory. Keep doing this week after week, month after month, year after year, and you can reach a level where you are considered a "really good" table tennis player.

How often should you train?

The players who improve the most are usually the players who train the most. These players can commit to playing 10-20 hours of table tennis per week. So, the answer is simple, isn't it? If you want to improve - and quickly - you also need to spend 10-20 hours per week hitting balls. But here's the problem. Committing to 10-20 hours of practice per week is unrealistic for most amateur table tennis players. We have jobs, or we're in full-time education, or we have caring responsibilities. There are not enough hours in the day. Or for many of us, our bodies simply can't take that much activity. We'd be permanently injured.

So, what is the ideal amount of time to train, when you don't have much time to train? Ideally, you should aim for at least one training session per week, playing for 1-2 hours. This is the minimum you need for a steady and slow rate of improvement. If you can manage two training sessions - 2-4 hours per week - then your improvement will be quicker. If you can train even more than this - let's say 4-10 hours - then you can improve faster still. It depends on your existing commitments and whether there are actually venues available to train several hours per week. If you are fortunate enough to be able to train for 10-20 hours, then fantastic! You will improve a lot quicker than I have.

In all the years I have been playing table tennis, I have averaged 2-4 hours of training per week. It's not much, which may explain my slow rate of improvement. With work, children and then my coaching career, my training time has been squeezed, but I have always tried to do some training every week.

Do what training you can, knowing that any training is better than none. The more important factor is the regularity of your training. Ideally, this means training every week - even if it's just for one hour. To develop a new serve, a new shot or to improve existing technique, you need regular practice. You need to reinforce the new skill until it forms part of your muscle memory. Only when you can play a shot without thinking, are you likely to be able to use it in a match effectively. To develop a skill to this level is really hard to do if you have long gaps between training sessions. The pathways in your brain never get deep enough to retain the new skill. Players who only train now and then tend to stall. They can maintain their existing skills, but they find it really difficult to develop new skills. They stay at the same level.

The best players in any club aren't usually the most naturally talented (whatever that means). They are usually the players who just keep turning up week after week. It's the same with me. I'm one of the stronger players in my club, but this isn't due to some inherent talent I was born with. I just keep turning up. Over the past 13 years, I have very rarely skipped a week of training. Every week 1, 2, 3 or 4 hours of training. It all adds up. The skills become embedded in my muscle memory.

Summer training

A good example of this is summer. My favourite time of the year. It's also the time of the year when many people have a break from playing table tennis. This is completely understandable. There are fewer leagues and tournaments. The weather is good. People want to be outdoors and do other activities. Often people are away for holidays. And some people just like to take a complete break from playing table tennis for a while and the summer seems the best time to do it.

However, I have always loved training throughout the summer. Clubs tend to be quieter, so I get more table time. It always seems like a good opportunity to do some quality practice. There are no league matches, so I can really focus on making improvements to my game. I work on areas of my game which will make a difference when the league season starts. This could be working on a strength and making it even stronger. Or it could be working on a weakness – something which is losing me points when I play.

And every year, when summer turns to autumn, and the absent players return to the club, I always feel that my level is higher than a few months before. I have improved. The returning players are the same as before. Multiply this over several summers and it partially helps to explain why I have improved a lot more compared to other players who were once the same level as me.

Focus on training regularly

It would be easy for me to say that you should train for twenty hours per week. Of course that would be great. It is stating the obvious. The more hours you train the more you can improve. But I have never been able to do this level of training as an adult with a full-time job and family. It just hasn't been feasible. Even though I have trained much less - only 2-4 hours per week - I have still been able to improve.

Don't worry too much about how many hours you train. As long as you train with a purpose, you can make good use of any amount of maintain the rally for as long. Five, six, seven backhands and then the rally breaks down. They try playing a bit faster or with a bit more topspin, but the rally breaks down even faster. It's a little frustrating. They only spend five minutes playing backhand to backhand.

At this point, one of the player's decides he has had enough. He thanks his partner for playing and then seeks a new partner to play with. They have spent 30 minutes not really doing anything useful. Neither player has practised what they need to, but they have played a lot of forehand drives. This is often why people are very good at playing forehand drives because they practise it more than any other shot.

I was certainly guilty of training this way when I started playing in London. Everyone else seemed to do it too. I was just copying them and trying to fit in, but I soon came to the conclusion that I was wasting my time. I only had limited opportunities to train, and I wanted to make better use of my time. Hitting forehand to forehand is just one tiny aspect of table tennis. As I outlined at the beginning of this chapter, there is a huge list of skills you need to master to be a very good all-round player. In reality, it's very rare that we play forehand to forehand rallies in a match for more than a couple of balls. One of the players will usually change the direction of play. So hitting forehand to forehand, or backhand to backhand, for too long in training sessions seems a bit of a pointless exercise.

It is much better to train with a more specific purpose. You should work on something which will help improve your game. This could be anything. A specific shot - push, block, flick, loop or smash. Serve and third ball. Returning serves. Switching between forehand and backhand strokes. Attacking backspin balls. Playing with more speed, more spin or more power. You might want to develop a strength or improve a weakness. It doesn't matter what you choose, as long as it is relevant to your game and will help you improve.

Let's keep things simple. If you are like me, you probably have loads of things you need to work on. But if you try to focus on too many things at once, you are in danger of not doing anything well. Instead, for each training session, just focus on one skill you want to improve. Just one. This will allow you to have a deep focus on that skill. You will learn more and improve faster.

For example, I want to improve my backhand flick. It's a shot I sometimes use when I play, but I want to be more consistent. This is my top priority. If I feel confident that I can execute my backhand flick with high consistency, then I am more likely to use this shot in a competitive match. I would also like to increase the speed and spin of the flick - as long as I can maintain high consistency. Lastly, I want to improve my recovery after the flick, so if the ball is returned I can attack the next ball too.

Back in the training hall, I have a quick knock-up with my partner. A little forehand to forehand, and backhand to backhand, to loosen up and get a feel for the ball and the table. But then I stop. I ask my partner if it's OK if we practise something in particular. I have never had a partner say no to this request. I explain what I would like to practise and put on a timer for seven minutes. And off we go.

I like to keep my drills simple. I get my partner to serve short backspin to the backhand half of the table. I then execute my backhand flick. After this the rally is open and both of us can try to win the point. After seven minutes, I ask my partner if there is anything he would like to work on. Sometimes he may choose the same drill. Sometimes something completely different. When his turn is finished, I can work on my backhand flick again. I may do the same drill or tweak it slightly to make it a little harder.

After 30 minutes, both myself and my partner have worked on one area of our game, which needs improving and will actually make a positive impact in a match situation. With this more focused training approach I have worked on the following:

- Reading the amount of backspin on the serve
- Footwork moving into the table
- Adjusting my bat angle to counter the amount of backspin
- The motion of the backhand flick
- Using my wrist to generate more spin
- Effective ball placement of my backhand flick
- Footwork out of the table having played my flick
- Recovery position for the next shot
- Watching my opponent to see where the next ball will go
- Trying to dominate the rally with the 4th ball
- Strategies to win the point

This is much more useful than aimlessly hitting the ball forehand to forehand. I am actually developing a skill which can really make a significant difference in a match situation. Even though my focus was on one skill - the backhand flick - I am actually training multiple different skills which are essential for random play and winning points. The training may be a little messier compared to playing forehand to forehand. The rallies are shorter. There are more errors. But the learning is much better and more relevant to match-play. I am trying to develop a skill which will help me win more points and reach a higher level. This is purposeful practice.

Try to have a focus for each training session. You might have a few areas of your game that you switch between every training session. One week, the backhand flick. The next week, serve and 3rd ball. The next week, your forehand loop. Or if you are really trying to master one skill, then you might focus on it again and again until you are really happy with your progress. It doesn't matter how you approach this, as long as you have some focus for each training session. You don't have to spend all of your training session working on a specific skill. Absolutely not. You don't want to suck all the life out of your training session and make it too serious. Allow time for some unstructured random play. Have some fun too. Table tennis should be fun. This is why we all play, but get that balance right. Feel as though you have progressed a part of your game each training session. Keep developing your skills. Do this purposeful practice week after week, year after year and you will keep on improving.

Three training methods

Hopefully I have convinced you of the benefits of training every week and training with a purpose. Now, we are going to look at what you actually do in a training session. There are three main types of training method:

1. Regular training drills - these are exercises where you know where the ball is going to go, e.g. two balls to your forehand, two balls to your backhand.
2. Irregular training drills - these are exercises where you don't always know where the ball is going to go, e.g. one or two balls to your forehand, one or two balls to your backhand.
3. Match-play - this could be serve and receive exercises or just playing matches.

Which type of training method should you focus on? Which option will help you improve the most? Let's look at each option.

Regular training drills

Regular drills, where you know where the ball is going, are really useful for developing technique. They are essential for beginners and intermediate players who are learning how to play. Regular drills are also important for advanced players to maintain the quality of their technique, develop their technique further and learn new shots.

The reason is simple. If you don't need to worry about where the ball is going, you can really focus on the technique. If I want to learn how to do a backhand loop, it's much easier if I receive a backspin ball in the same position with roughly the same amount of spin. I can then focus on the mechanics of the shot - the backswing, the wrist, the swing trajectory, the contact and the follow through. I don't have to worry about footwork, watching my opponent or trying to win a point. I can just focus on the execution. If the play was more random, then it would be significantly more difficult to learn the shot.

Another example. Let's say I want to improve switching between backhand and forehand drives. I get my partner to give me one ball to my backhand and one ball to my forehand. Again, I can really focus on this specific skill - the footwork, changing the bat angle between forehand and backhand, and hitting the ball at the top of the bounce. I can get really good at this skill, if I know where the ball is going and I don't have to deal with randomness and trying to win the point.

Regular drills are really useful for players of all standards. We all like doing these drills. They are easy to do. They make us feel good and look good. But there can be a downside. If you spend all your time doing regular drills - at the expense of other training methods - you may actually harm your overall game.

I'm sure you know the sort of player. He looks amazing in the training hall, hitting beautiful backhands and forehands, but he always seems to do the same fixed training routines. Forehand to forehand, backhand to backhand and footwork exercises switching between forehand and backhand. He knows where the ball is going, moves effortlessly into position, plays his shot, then moves to the next position and plays the next shot. This player often has excellent looking technique, but when it comes to playing matches, he struggles. Why is this?

By heavily focusing on regular drills, this player is learning the mechanics of the shots he uses, but there are many things he is not learning which are vital for match-play - reading spin, reacting to random placement and learning how to win points. Essentially, he is learning a dance routine. Move feet here. Rotate there. Contact ball now. Move feet here. Hit ball there and repeat. Whilst this set routine can look aesthetically pleasing, it's not really table tennis. When he plays a match, everything is different. The ball doesn't go to a set position, at a set pace and set spin. It's random. Random placement, random spin, random speed. His skills at dealing with randomness are underdeveloped. This seemingly excellent looking player turns out to be quite weak.

Regular drills are vital for developing technique, but you don't want to spend all your time doing these types of drills. You also need other training methods.

Irregular training drills

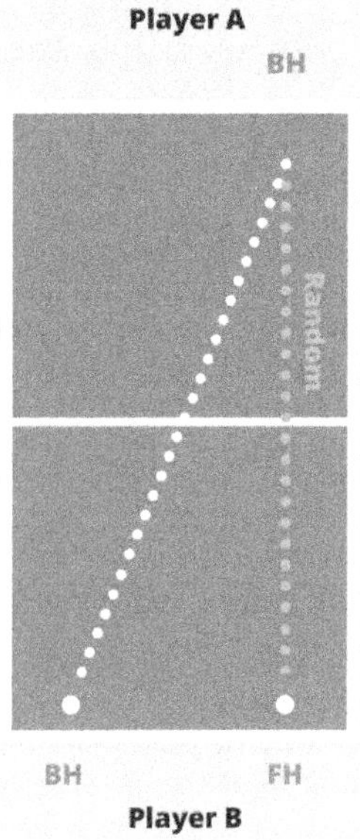

Irregular drills are more complex. These are drills with some element of randomness. You don't always know where the ball is going to go.

A simple example is playing backhand to backhand, but Player A - the controller - can switch the ball to Player B's forehand whenever he chooses, as shown in the diagram. Player B has to read this switch, move into position, play a forehand down the line and then the rally continues backhand to backhand until the next switch. In this exercise there is a small, but very important element of randomness. Player B has to stay alert - just like in a match. He has to really watch his opponent - just like in a match. He has to move and transition from backhand to forehand whilst under pressure - just like in a match. He is developing the skills needed to perform well in the randomness of a match.

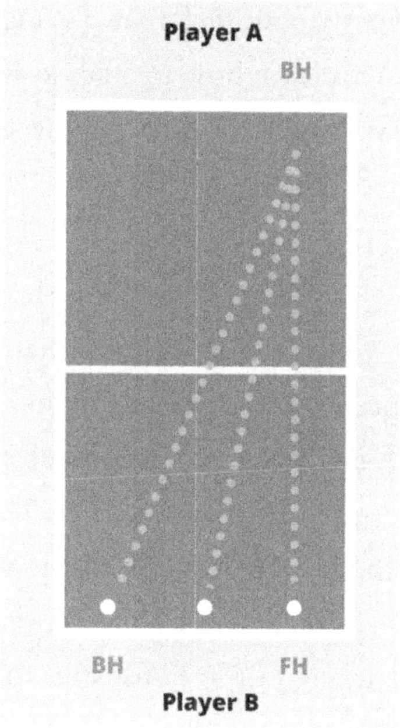

Another classic example. Player B plays forehand and backhand topspins to Player A's backhand. Player A - the controller - can block the ball to any position on the table. Player B has to react to balls which may come to his forehand, his backhand or the middle of the table, in any order. Once again there is randomness - more than the previous example. Every ball is potentially played to a different position on the table. Player B has to use all his concentration, footwork and rallying skills to keep the drill going. He is once again developing skills to cope with randomness - skills he will need when he plays matches.

Irregular drills are generally harder than regular drills. You feel more pressure. You make more errors. But they are vital. It's a way to stress-test your technique. You soon identify whether your technique is match-ready. For example, I find it quite easy to play forehand loops in an irregular drill. My technique can withstand the pressure of randomness.

My backhand loop, however, tends to break down. I make too many errors, which is an indication that I need to practise my backhand loop more, before I'll be able to use it consistently and effectively in matches.

Irregular drills help prepare you for the randomness of matches, but they also have limitations. A drill is a drill. Your aim is to develop a skill in a controlled - albeit pressured - scenario. Irregular drills don't fully prepare you for the intricacies of playing and winning points. You don't learn about different playing styles. You don't learn match tactics. You don't learn how to analyse an opponent and implement a game plan. To develop these skills you need another training method.

Match-play

Match-play includes exercises involving a serve, a return of serve and playing out a point. It could involve an element of regularity, e.g. Player A always serves short backspin to Player B's backhand. Player B always does a backhand flick to Player A's backhand and then the rally is free and both players try to win the point.

Or it could involve more irregularity, e.g. Player A serves either short backspin or long topspin to Player B's backhand. Player B either flicks or drives to Player A's backhand and then the rally is free and both players try to win the point. Or it could involve just playing matches. No conditions attached. Just a normal game, up to 11 points.

When you do match-play training, you develop additional areas of your game. These include:

- Match tactics
- Learning to play against different styles

- Using serves effectively
- Returning a variety of different serves
- Winning points
- Dealing with pressure

These are skills you need to develop to win table tennis matches. At amateur level table tennis, you will often see a player who looks quite average and unorthodox – who can barely keep a rally going in a warm-up – but can still easily beat a player with seemingly far superior technique. The ugly looking player may not have great-looking strokes, but by doing lots of match-play training, he has learnt how to use his strokes tactically, how to serve effectively, how to return serves, how to deal with the randomness and how to win matches.

Some players avoid match-play in training sessions. Some find it too confrontational. Others want to protect their ego. They don't want to risk losing, fearing they will move down some imaginary pecking order. But by never playing practice matches, they never really learn how to win competitive matches. All the regular and irregular training drills they do, only partially prepares them for competition. There is a key piece of the puzzle missing. Their tactical skills are underdeveloped.

Match-play training is essential. Don't worry whether you win or lose. Who cares if you lose more points than your partner? It's only training. Instead, approach each match-play exercise as a learning opportunity. This could be trying to serve in a certain way, return in a certain way, trying to topspin rather than push, trying to move your feet better or whatever the priority is for you. It's an opportunity to experiment, try out new tactics or use new shots you have been developing in your regular and irregular training drills.

I often train with a player called Martin Gray, who has been ranked in the top 50 in England. We have a short warm-up and then play lots of matches. Martin beats me every single time we play, but sometimes I get close. I find these practice matches really useful. I get to play with a high-quality opponent. I learn from my many errors. I learn to play more positively - I have to, otherwise he destroys me. I learn new tactics. I learn how to serve with more spin. I learn how to take risks. I learn how to play table tennis at a higher level. It keeps me sharp and makes me a better player overall.

Find your balance

Good quality training should involve all three training methods - regular drills, irregular drills and match-play. Regular drills help you maintain and develop technique and learn new shots. Irregular drills help you cope with randomness. Match-play helps you develop your tactics and point winning strategies.

How much you do of each training method is up to you. I have always liked playing matches in training. It gets me really motivated and engaged. I enjoy the competitive edge. I like testing my skills in a completely random scenario. I like experimenting with different playing styles and tactics. I probably devote at least 50% of my training time to playing matches. However, this amount of match-play does come at a cost. My technique is often lacking (more on this in the next chapter). My footwork is weak. I'm not an elegant looking player! But I do know how to win points and matches. However, I know other top division local league players who approach training the other way around. They will do mostly regular and irregular drills (80%) and a little less match-play (20%), and also play at a very high level. Despite the different ratios, they still use - and benefit from - all three training methods.

You might use different ratios depending on the time of year. During the summer months, when I am not competing, I tend to do more regular and irregular drills. I work on improving my technique. But as a league season approaches, I will increase my match-play training. I want to get sharp for the first league matches.

So, you choose the ratio. And the ratio is completely flexible. You decide how much of each training method you need to do, depending on what your priorities are. As long as you use all three methods, you will get maximum benefit from your training.

Your training plan

I have discussed many ideas in this chapter. Let's put it all together and create a training plan for the next four weeks. The first step is to work out how often you can train. This will obviously be determined by your existing commitments and what options are actually available to train. Do you have access to a club with an open practice evening? Can you hire a table in a sports centre and train with a partner? Can you take some 1-to-1 coaching sessions? Do you have a robot you could use? Are there any group coaching sessions you can participate in? These are all good training options. Make sure you have at least one training session per week. If you want to stretch yourself, add some extra sessions in. Here's my schedule:

Week 1

- Tuesday: Club practice night (2 hours)
- Thursday: 1-to-1 coaching session (1 hour)

Week 2

- Tuesday: Club practice night (2 hours)
- Friday: Practise with robot (1 hour)

Week 3

- Tuesday: Club practice night (2 hours)
- Wednesday: Practise with partner at sports centre (2 hours)

Week 4

- Tuesday: Club practice night (2 hours)
- Saturday: Group coaching session (2 hours)

I plan to do 14 hours of training over the next four weeks, using a few different options. Normally, I would just attend the club practice night, but this month I have decided to stretch myself and do some more training. I'm eager to improve!

Next, think about the purpose of your training. What three skills will really make a difference to your game right now? This could be anything. Improving your technique, learning a new shot, developing an existing serve, improving your footwork, reading service spin - anything. You might want to work on a weakness or develop a strength. Whatever you choose, make it very relevant to your game. Table tennis is an individual sport. Your priorities need to make sense to you.

Here are my priorities for the next four weeks:

1. Backhand flick - I can play this shot already, but I want to develop it further by generating more speed and spin.

2. Backhand loop - I struggle with this shot. I can do it in a regular drill, but I struggle when the play is more random. I want to get more consistent.
3. Returning serves - An ongoing issue. I lose too many points when returning serves. I want to improve my ability to read spin and just get the ball back on the table.

These three skills are directly related to match-play. If I can improve all three, I will be able to win more points. I plan to work on all three over the next four weeks. I'm not going to plan too far in advance when I will work on each skill. I will take a flexible approach to each training session, but for each training session, I am definitely going to work on one of these skills.

Finally, plan how you are going to practise each skill during your training sessions. You can use regular drills, irregular drills and match-play. You don't need to plan loads of drills. Just one or two for each skill should be enough. Don't overcomplicate the drills. Simple is often best.

Here are some ideas for improving my backhand flick:

1. Regular / match-play drill - My partner serves short backspin to the middle of the backhand side. I play a backhand flick to any position. The play is now open, and we both try to win the point.
2. Irregular / match-play drill - My partner serves short to any position. If to my forehand, I shall play a forehand push. If to my backhand or the middle, I will play a backhand flick. I can return to any position. The play is now open, and we both try to win the point.

3. Match-play - Normal game up to 11. However, if the serve is short to the backhand or middle, I have to play a backhand flick. I am not allowed to play a backhand push.

.

With exercise 1, I am improving the quality of my backhand flick. I know where the ball will be served, so I can focus on the mechanics of the stroke. With exercise 2, I am using my improved backhand flick in a random scenario. I have to watch my opponent closely and react quickly, whilst still trying to execute a good quality backhand flick. With exercise 3, I am forcing myself to use my backhand flick in a practice match. This builds confidence. If I can execute my improved backhand flick in the complete randomness of a match, then I have greater confidence in using this shot when playing a real competitive match. My training has been successful.

You have seen my training plan. It's not complicated, but I have put some thought into it. I have increased my training hours. I have identified some key skills to develop. I have planned some drills.

I encourage you to do the same. Put this book down and get a piece of paper. Come up with a training plan for the next four weeks. You might not stick to it rigidly. That's fine. Life gets in the way sometimes. But by devising a plan, you are far more likely to do better quality training than if you have no plan at all.

Technique

Technique is a contentious issue. If you line up ten coaches and ask them how to do a backhand loop (or any stroke), you will most likely get ten different answers. How can this be? Surely there is a correct way of playing a shot and everything else is incorrect? Well no, not exactly. If only table tennis were that simple!

In this chapter, I'm *not* going to explain how to play various table tennis shots. I've tried following table tennis instruction manuals in the past, but I have never found them that helpful. It's difficult to truly understand the technique of a shot by reading a description and looking at a series of photos. I'm not going to waste your time or mine.

Fortunately, these days you can find video tutorials of every table tennis stroke for free on YouTube and other social media platforms. If you want to know how to play a particular shot, find a video online or, better still, ask a more advanced player or a coach. Seeing a technique in action is much better than reading a description in a book.

This chapter is not about teaching you technique. Instead, I will encourage you to think about technique differently. I won't provide you with many answers, but challenge you to make up your own mind about the importance of technique, what technique is suitable for your game and whose technique you should aspire to.

My deficient technique

When I post a coaching video on my YouTube channel, I always have a sense of trepidation. Usually my videos are received well, especially by beginner and intermediate players, to whom my videos are mainly aimed. But I often get a few comments, where my technique is completely trashed. I get told I do this wrong, and that wrong, and I should try to play the shot like the best professionals, usually someone from the Chinese National Team. It can be a brutal experience.

I once posted a coaching video on how to play a forehand loop. Here are some comments I received:

- "I see severe deficiency in technique."
- "The biggest problem you have here is you're using your arm / forearm to power the shot."
- "Please take a look at the Chinese players…how they use their legs, waist and weight transfer."
- "There are a number of errors in your loop. First, bend down from the waist. Second, the non-playing hand cannot be away from the playing hand. Third, the racket tip must be downward, while looping. And, the last but not the least, the head must not be far away from the racket."

- "You are going up and not forwards. Against backspin, you need to contact the ball at peak or just after and then go forwards (so that the ball does not sit up after bounce on the other side)."
- "The Chinese technique is better."
- "No offence intended (really), but you need to take some lessons."

Ouch. The truth can hurt sometimes. I get this type of feedback on many of my videos. Moving away from keyboard warriors on the internet into the real world, the situation is pretty much the same. I don't actually recall receiving much glowing feedback about my technique from other coaches. Just a sigh and a general resignation that there is a lot of work needed to get my technique into better shape. My flicks, my loops, my stance, my footwork, my grip, my backhand - it all needs work. I have never been a role model for others to copy. When people see me play, I think the reaction is one of surprise. Surprise that I can actually win matches in the top division of a local league.

So, the big question: if my technique is deficient, how come I've done OK? How come I have been able to progress through the divisions? How come I have been able to turn my passion into a career and people from all parts of the UK travel and pay to have coaching with me? The truth is that technique is just one aspect of what makes a player effective. There are other factors which are equally important – match tactics, ball placement, playing style, shot variation, mindset and working out your opponent's strengths and weaknesses.

I have seen many players over the years with seemingly excellent form and technique. They really play their drives and topspin shots well. They move effortlessly and efficiently. They transfer their body weight superbly. They are a joy to watch, but they are rubbish at table tennis matches. How come? Usually because their skills are severely underdeveloped in other areas. They don't understand tactics. They struggle to return serves. They don't know how to play against unusual playing styles. They crumble under pressure.

I have also seen many players whose technique looks absolutely shocking. Jerky movements. Inefficient stroke actions. No weight transfer. Horrible, ugly and messy, but they have really high win percentages. Even though their strokes look a bit weird, they can play them consistently. And they are usually very advanced in other areas - match tactics, service, mindset. They know how to win points. They know how to play table tennis.

Of course, if you want to be the number one player in the world, your technique needs to be pretty damn amazing and faultless. But if you have more modest goals – to be one of the best players in your club or your league or win a local amateur tournament, you do not need professional standard technique.

As for me, I actually think my technique is OK. It's consistent. It's usable. I have confidence in my technique. It's certainly not professional standard. This is why I play at an amateur level. But I am realistic. I am 40-years-old. I started playing late. I have lots of bad habits to fix. I'm never going to be a really smooth player with amazing technique. I still want to improve my technique - increase my speed, spin and power. This is absolutely important, but so is improving my tactics, my mental game, my physical fitness, my understanding of playing styles, my consistency, my ball placement and my ability to read spin. Technique is important for overall improvement, but it's just one of many important factors.

What is 'correct' technique?

I don't subscribe to the idea that there is one true way of playing any table tennis stroke. Be wary of the player or coach who tells you that *you must* play a shot in a certain way and no other. They are usually talking nonsense. In reality, there are different ways that you can play every shot in table tennis and still achieve a high level of consistency and effectiveness.

Let's take a forehand loop as an example. Your opponent has given you some nasty backspin. It could be a push, a chop, or a backspin serve. You feel positive and decide to execute a forehand loop attack. When playing this forehand loop, you could:

- Use a more horizontal swing with a straighter arm and a lot of body weight transfer
- Use a more vertical swing with a bent arm and less body weight transfer
- Use a much shorter swing, with hardly any use of legs or waist

For the arc of the ball, you could:

- Spin the ball high over the net
- Spin the ball low over the net

- Hook the ball with topspin and sidespin

For the speed and spin of the shot, you could:

- Play slow and spinny
- Faster and flatter
- Somewhere in between

Which is the best option? Which is most likely to win you the point? I imagine you would like me to give you a definitive answer, but I can't. It depends on your playing style, physical conditioning, body shape, age and the equipment you use.

I train with two players at my club in Cambridge - Mirek and Martin. Both are very good players. Both are very different players. Mirek likes to play back from the table with long, elegant strokes. For his forehand loop, he uses a very horizontal swing, a straight arm and lots of weight transfer. The ball comes over the net low, with a lot of speed and spin. We could call this the Chinese method, as this is how players from China are taught to play a forehand loop. By comparison, Martin stays closer to the table, with more compact strokes. Martin plays a forehand loop with a shorter stroke. His swing is more vertical and his arm is more bent throughout the stroke. The ball comes over the net slower with a higher arc but is loaded with topspin. We could call this the European method, as it is a more commonly taught technique in European countries.

Which is correct? Since Chinese players dominate professional table tennis, you could argue that the Chinese method is best. This may be the case at the very top of the professional game, but at amateur level it doesn't really matter. Both Mirek and Martin have very different forehand loops, but both are consistent. Both are effective. Both win lots of points. Both have a forehand loop technique which works for their playing style. Both techniques are hugely effective at amateur level. Both are correct.

Consistent and effective

The 'correct' forehand loop technique is the one you can do consistently and effectively. If your forehand loop is consistent, this means you can attack pushes, chops and backspin serves again and again with few errors. Consistency gives you confidence. Consistency keeps the ball on the table. Consistency increases your chances of winning a point. But consistency isn't always enough. It is also important that your forehand loop is effective and offers a threat. Your forehand loop should be able to put your opponent under pressure or win a point outright. This could be a faster and flatter loop. It could also be a slower and very spinny loop. If your forehand loop wins you points, then it is effective. Your forehand loop may not be pro-standard. Other people may tell you that you are doing it wrong. But if you have a consistent and effective forehand loop - no matter what technique you use - then you can say it is 'correct' for your game.

The forehand loop is not the only shot you can play in different ways. *Every* table tennis shot - flick, drive, push, block, chop, smash - you can play in different ways. Players are always searching for the 'correct' way. Coaches are always championing their 'correct' way, but I just don't believe a one-size-fits-all 'correct' way exists for any table tennis stroke.

There are multiple options and nuances for every shot. Your task is to find a way to play every table tennis stroke consistently and effectively.

During your table tennis journey you will receive lots of advice from other players and from coaches. Sometimes the advice will be consistent. Sometimes the advice will be contradictory. You need to experiment. Try out different ideas and methods. Some technique advice will instantly work for you. Other advice will feel like it has come from an alien planet! Adopt the advice which enhances your technique. Ignore the advice, no matter how well-intentioned, which seems to make you worse. Judge your technique by how consistent and effective it is. These are your two measures. Is your stroke consistent? Can you play the stroke again and again without error? Is your stroke effective? Does your stroke win points or put your opponent under pressure? If your answer is 'yes' to these questions, you are doing something right with your technique.

Copying the professionals

How much should you try to copy professional table tennis players? Their technique is so smooth. Their footwork is brilliant. They can generate huge amounts of speed and spin. And they are incredibly accurate and consistent. Professional players make the game look easy and effortless. If we want to improve, then surely it makes sense to just study and copy what the professional players do? Well, yes and no.

I recently watched a video of Japanese superstar Tomokazu Harimoto doing some hard training. In the video Harimoto hit lots of phenomenal forehand topspins. His waist rotation is massive. During his backswing, you can see his bat way behind his body. His racket speed is exceptionally fast. His footwork is lightning speed. He is generating huge amounts of spin. And almost every forehand he hits lands on the table. It's beautiful to watch, but it's also incredibly difficult to do.

There are at least ten elements to the stroke that he is executing perfectly for it to work:

- Foot position
- Stance
- Weight transfer
- Backswing
- Forward swing trajectory

- Bat angle
- Timing
- Contact point on the ball
- Finish position
- Recovery

I'm sure the list could be much longer, but if any of these elements are sub-standard (e.g. same swing, but with a more upright stance), then his shot quality would be less and his consistency would drop.

To play table tennis in this extreme way - and still be very consistent - takes huge amounts of training and physical conditioning, plus the benefit of having a young supple body. When we amateur players try to emulate such high-level technique, but without putting in the same amount of training (which for most of us is impossible as we have jobs, studies or family responsibilities), then consistency can be very low.

And consistency is essential. If you try to copy the forehand topspin technique of Tomokazu Harimoto, but only manage to get one in ten on the table, then it's not much use. The one shot you successfully execute may be amazing - and you'll get a few claps and high praise from anyone watching - but if you miss the next nine attempts, then you'll be losing a lot more points than you win. So, it's not a good shot.

Trying to copy professional players exactly is very hard to do, without putting in a sufficient amount of training. I experience this sometimes in a coaching session. I will be coaching a player who tries to execute wild forehands - big backswings, fast racket speed and lots of physical energy - but will miss far more than actually land on the table.

We usually stop and have a chat. I ask the player why he (it is almost always a 'he') plays his forehand topspins like this. The player will reply that this is how Ma Long / Xu Xin / Fan Zhendong / Tomokazu Harimoto (delete as appropriate) does it. I will then ask the player how often he trains. The players will usually say 2-4 hours per week. I then highlight how much a professional player trains by comparison and try to convince him that trying to copy exactly the forehand topspin technique of Ma Long (or whoever) may not be very useful.

We then try to tone down the technique a bit. We use some key elements of how a professional player may execute a forehand topspin, but not to such an extreme level. We use waist rotation - but not as much as a professional. We maintain good racket speed - but not as much as a professional. We try to engage the legs - but not as much as a professional. The result is a very decent forehand topspin shot which is more controlled, but far more consistent. A shot which is capable of actually winning more points than it loses.

Usable technique

Developing good quality, and usable, shots is the key for amateur players with limited time to train. It's great to watch professional players. And we can try to emulate some of what they do, but we need to be realistic about what is possible. We have to appreciate that the reason professional players are amazing is because of the huge amounts of training they do. Without putting in similar levels of training it is hard to play such high-level table tennis with any kind of consistency.

We should recognise that professional players push their technique to the limits, to maximise the speed and spin of their shots. They need to do this to be competitive at the highest levels. They need power to win points. Lots of it. At the amateur level we don't need anywhere near as much explosive power to win points. A moderately fast attack, with good ball placement, is usually sufficient. We don't need to push our bodies to the limit.

So yes, watch professional players and learn from them. Try to emulate them to some extent. But to succeed in amateur table tennis it is not necessary to copy *exactly* the technique of professional players. Consistent, effective and usable technique is usually good enough.

Unorthodox technique

Let's move on to unorthodox technique. This is not a widely discussed topic, but let's face it, at amateur level table tennis, unorthodox technique is everywhere. There are many players who have strange strokes. Shots which seem to defy the laws of physics. The arm jerks and the bat twitches, but somehow the ball lands on the table, leaving you completely bewildered. How on earth is that shot possible? We all know the sort of player. I'm sure you have an unorthodox shot or two. I know I do! So, is unorthodox technique OK? Can unorthodox technique be an advantage? Or should we avoid it at all costs?

Unorthodox technique means playing a shot in a way which is different from the generally accepted norm. It could be a little different or it could deviate from the norm massively. It usually occurs when players teach themselves to play table tennis. With no coach to guide them, they develop their own strange-looking strokes. As a coach, I try to remain open-minded about unorthodox technique. This is because unorthodox technique can be highly effective at amateur level, so long as the strokes can be executed consistently.

Let me introduce you to my team-mate Yordan. We have been playing together for many years. We started together in the bottom division in Cambridge. And we have stayed together, moving up the divisions and winning the top division for the past two years. Yordan is the king of unorthodox technique. His grip is wrong. His stance is wrong. His footwork is wrong. His forehand topspin technique is wrong.

His service action is weird. He blocks funny. His pushes are odd. He can't loop. He can't flick. Yet somehow, Yordan wins a lot. He is an absolute pain to play against.

I once thought Yordan needed to change his entire game, to become more orthodox, because that's the 'best' way to play table tennis. But why? It's his unorthodox technique which causes opponents so many problems. Higher ranked players struggle against him and juniors are completely flummoxed. They're not used to the way he plays. They have no visual blueprint to make sense of his shots. They haven't developed tactics to beat him. I have seen full-grown men have meltdowns because they can't work him out. They just can't believe they can lose to someone who plays such weird shots like Yordan.

I have the benefit of playing with Yordan fairly regularly and I have got used to his shots. But because he's mastered his unorthodox technique, it's still hard work. He wins half. I win half. No one else I know plays like him. That's the advantage he brings to every match.

Benefit of unorthodox technique

Unorthodox technique can be an advantage. It can be difficult for an opponent to read the spin, trajectory and placement, if the shot is different to the norm. Table tennis is so fast, you don't have time to think. You have to react in a fraction of a second to the shot your opponent has played. To do this well, you have to train your skills over a long period of time until they become automatic. Then you can subconsciously read the cues of your opponent and react accordingly. An unorthodox stroke disrupts this process. If you don't have a visual blueprint for an unorthodox stroke, you may hesitate or panic or prod at the ball. It unsettles you. You have not seen the technique before. You are not quite sure what to do.

I have a player I coach, Stuart, who has an unorthodox forehand drive technique. Very little backswing and he twists his bat over mid-stroke. It's a stroke he has made up himself. No one has coached him to play this stroke. No one would coach *anyone* else to play this stroke, but somehow it works for Stuart. It is really hard to read where the ball is going to go.

I'm very good at blocking. I spend many hours each week blocking other player's shots. If a player has conventional forehand technique, I can block all day long. I can see from the shape of the body and the swing trajectory where the ball is going before the player has hit the ball. I have the visual blueprint to understand the shot. I can react very quickly, as I have witnessed the movement many thousands of times before. But I struggle against Stuart. He regularly catches me out. He is the only player I know who plays his forehand in this way. I have far less visual memory to help me recognise the specific cues of when he will hit down the line or when he will hit cross-court. If I were to play with Stuart for thousands of hours, I would get used to it, but I only coach him 2-3 hours per month. So, I'm still struggling.

This is the major benefit of an unorthodox stroke. In a competitive match, your opponent has little time to get used to it and adjust accordingly. The unorthodox player has a head start and the opponent may never catch-up.

Of course, if a player's technique is too unorthodox, it can limit how much the player can progress. There aren't any players competing at the top of the sport with crazy unorthodox technique. Yordan would find it difficult to progress beyond the local league level with his unorthodox technique. He would need to smooth out some of his weirdness. But at local league level and amateur competitions it is possible to have success with unorthodox technique, as long as the strokes can be executed with high consistency.

We are back to that key word 'consistency' again. This is vital. Unorthodox technique is really only effective if it's consistent. If you have an unorthodox shot which rarely lands on the table, it's probably not worth persevering with it. You would be better off learning conventional technique. But if you have unorthodox shots, which you are confident in playing, and are highly consistent, then stick with it. You really don't have to change your game to be more like everyone else. An unorthodox player has the advantage of the surprise factor, which can be very effective at amateur level.

Improving your technique

Having read through this chapter, you may think I don't place that much value on excellent technique. This is a strange position to take as a table tennis coach. I suppose I am just a bit more relaxed about technique. I have lost to enough players with strange technique, and beaten enough players with supposedly correct technique, to know that technique is just one element which makes up a decent table tennis player.

But technique *is* important - of course it is. And we should absolutely try to improve our technique in our training sessions. The goal doesn't have to be perfection, but a continual drive for improvement will make you a better player. To play in a higher division or to go further in a tournament, you will need to keep improving your technique. You may need more spin, more speed, better accuracy, higher levels of consistency or add a new shot to your game. Whatever your focus, improving your technique will make a difference. But how do you go about improving your technique? What's the best method?

In Chapter 3, I talked about different training methods - regular drills (where you know where the ball is going), irregular drills (where you don't know where the ball is going) and match-play. When trying to improve your technique, it is best to start with regular training drills. It's difficult to make changes and achieve consistency in random play. With regular drills you can focus solely on the mechanics of a shot. You then need a lot of repetition until the change in your technique becomes automatic. If you are trying to make a small technique change, you may not need that much repetition. If it's a big change, or a new shot, you may need huge amounts of repetition.

My forehand strokes come quite naturally to me. When I make a tweak to my forehand technique, I can usually make the change quite quickly. My backhand is a different story. My backhand is not natural. I have to work much harder on my backhand technique to get it into a usable state. I have been working on my backhand drive for ten years and it's still a bit hit-and-miss! It does take time.

Multi-ball training is very useful for developing technique. This is where a coach or another player will feed you a lot of balls and you keep repeating a shot over and over again. This repetition helps create the pathways in your brain, so you can execute a shot without thinking, relying solely on your muscle memory.

A table tennis robot is also useful and something I have used a lot. I have always felt slightly bad asking a coach or a player to feed multi-ball. It's a bit boring for the feeder. But a robot doesn't have feelings. It can feed you balls for hours and hours and not get bored. It doesn't matter how many mistakes you make. The robot doesn't get frustrated or make judgements. It just keeps giving you balls to hit.

It can be tempting to give up on a technique change if you don't get instant success. But if you really believe the technique change will make a difference, then you just have to keep persevering. It takes time and a lot of effort, but all this repetition is necessary to develop your muscle memory and high levels of consistency.

When you are happy with your technique in regular drills, then move on to irregular drills and then finally to match-play. Old habits tend to appear when the pressure is on. If you can successfully use your new and improved technique in a pressure situation, you know you have mastered it.

Coaching and observation

Another way I have improved my technique over the years is through coaching. I have attended many coaching camps in the UK and Europe. These typically last 2-5 days and you get to play a lot of table tennis. There's usually a lot of training drills, focusing on technique, movement, service, returning serves and match-play. You also get access to multiple coaches, most of whom will have coached or played at a very high level. The coaches are always keen to share their knowledge, so you get exposed to different ideas and methods. You get individual feedback as you do the drills, and by the end of a training camp you have a big list of areas you can work on. Most of the training camps I have attended are heavily focused on technique, so they are a very good source of information and advice. Just do a quick internet search and you should find many training camp options for amateur players.

I have also had plenty of 1-to-1 coaching, mostly with Mark Mitchell, a former England player and more recently Ferenc Horvath, a top player from Hungary. Even though I am a full-time coach, I still get 1-to-1 coaching to develop my technique. Improvement should never stop. The great thing about 1-to-1 coaching is that the coach's attention is solely focused on you. A good coach should instantly be able to see which elements of a stroke needs to be improved to achieve more speed, spin or consistency. And you get instant feedback. It's a fast-track way to make rapid technique improvements. Every coach has different ideas and methods and will always be biased towards their own style of play. It's useful to try out different coaches and see which methods work best for you. I encourage players I coach to also have lessons with other coaches, just to get a different perspective. Often a player will come back with a new idea, which works for them, and enhances the work we do together.

Finally, another option, which is often neglected, is simple observation. Is there a player at your club who you admire and plays really well? Observe how this player executes his or her strokes. Where does the bat start? Where does the bat finish? What is the bat angle? What is the swing trajectory? Really pay attention. I have found it much more useful to observe a better player at a local club, rather than trying to copy a professional player online. It just seems more attainable, more realistic and more motivating. Plus it's much easier to ask questions. The club player is right there. The player will likely be flattered and will happily talk about his or her technique in great detail. You can learn a lot for free!

We have finished this chapter on a positive note. I have tried to reassure you that technique isn't all that matters at amateur level. You can still reach a high standard even if your technique is a bit weird. However, it is important to keep improving your technique and there are many ways you can do this. How much should you focus on technique? And how much should you focus on other aspects of your game? This is for you to decide. But the 'other aspects of the game' is where we will now switch our attention. And for me, this is where the fun really starts. Next up… service.

Service

If I seemed relaxed about technique in the previous chapter, I am going to be far more passionate about service. Serves matter a lot, especially in amateur table tennis. The quality of your serves can make a significant difference to how many points you win in your matches.

Every point starts with a serve. When it's your serve, you have complete control. Your serve can help you win a cheap point, stop your opponent from attacking, set up a specific type of rally, or completely fool your opponent into making a weak return which you can smash away with a powerful third ball attack.

I have had team-mates over the years, whose overall games are not strong, but whose serves have been excellent. These players have achieved healthy win percentages based largely on winning points from their serves.

As for me, my service game has always been pretty decent. I have worked quite hard on my serves. Not just the service technique, but also the tactics of serving - when to use which serve, ball placement, and understanding how my serves are likely to be returned. In many games, when I have been struggling, it has been my serves which have won me points - giving me a little breathing space and helping me squeeze a victory. If you want to improve at table tennis, move up a division or progress further in a tournament, then improving your serves is a great place to start.

In this chapter, I will give you lots of practical tips on how to improve your service game. Once again, I must emphasise that this is not an instruction manual. I am not going to teach you service technique. I am not going to teach you new serves. Ask a coach, another player or look at videos online if you want new serves. Instead, I am going to focus on the serves you already use and how you can make them stronger. This is the quickest way to improve your service game. But first, let's just make sure we are all playing by the rules.

Illegal serves

One aspect of table tennis gets players more animated than any other - illegal serves. In local league table tennis illegal serves are very common. I've seen players argue, swear, throw chairs and threaten physical violence because of the questionable legality of a player's serve. Most of the time, players who serve illegally are unaware they are doing so. However, there are players who do it on purpose to gain an advantage. Umpires, who are often other players, rarely enforce the service rules. It's a bit of a mess.

The rules on service are a little ambiguous. The ball needs to be tossed 16 cm during service but this can be hard for an umpire to judge. The ball cannot be obscured by the server. The opponent must be able to see the ball. Again, this can be difficult for an umpire to judge, as the umpire does not have the same vantage point as the player receiving the serve. This is why players get into arguments.

I won't list the full service rules here, as I'm sure they will keep changing slightly over the years. For the latest service rules, just search on the International Table Tennis Federation website. But let's look at two rules which cause many heated arguments.

Ball toss and hidden serves

From my experience, the rule which is violated most often is not tossing the ball. Some players serve straight from the hand. This is not allowed. You have to toss the ball 16 cm and contact the ball as it is falling. 16 cm is not actually that high. It is roughly the height of the net or the height of the rubber on your table tennis bat.

The ball toss needs to be "near vertically". You shouldn't excessively toss the ball backwards or excessively toss the ball into your body. This rule is a bit vague. Umpires can have a different interpretation of "near vertically".

My advice is try to toss the ball vertically, but don't worry too much if it is a bit back or a bit sideways. I think a little backwards or sideways movement can be described as "near vertically", so this is within the rules.

Another rule which is often violated, especially at advanced and professional levels, is hiding the ball from your opponent when you serve. Typically, these players will use their upper body or arm to hide the contact with the ball. This makes it very hard for their opponents to see what type of spin is on the ball.

For the serve to be legal, your opponent needs to be able to see the ball throughout the service action. This means you have to keep the ball above the table, on an open palm. As you toss the ball, it falls and you contact it, you can't put any part of your body in the way to obscure the view of your opponent.

This rule can be difficult to judge. A service action can have a lot of movement with body and arms. You may not even be aware that a body part is obscuring the ball. My best advice is to film yourself from the perspective of your opponent. Watch the footage back. If you can see the ball at all times, your service action is legal. If your body obscures the ball, then you need to change your service action.

Do you have to serve legally?

If you only play for fun, in a social setting, and no one cares about the service rules, then it doesn't matter how you serve. As long as everyone in the room agrees, then serve however you want. But, if you play competitively, or aspire to play competitively, you really should serve legally. We want the game to be fair for all players. Win by the merit of your skills, not by playing by different rules.

There is a far more practical reason why you should try to serve legally. When I played in London, one of my team-mates had a pretty solid all-round game and would win most of his matches. But when he served he would never throw the ball up high enough. He was serving straight from his hand. Most of the time he would get away with it and dominate with his serve and a strong third ball attack.

However, sometimes an opponent would complain to the umpire. My team-mate then had to adjust his service technique by throwing the ball up. The problem was, his service was much weaker when he served legally. He just couldn't generate the same amount of spin. It's not that you can't generate lots of spin by serving legally (of course you can), it's just that he had never learnt to do it.

When he started serving legally, he wasn't able to dominate with his serve and third ball attack any more. His serve had gone from a strength to a weakness. This would affect the rest of his game too. As he relied on his illegal serves to win so many points, when this was taken away from him, he would often take too many risks with the rest of his game. He would make lots of unforced errors. His game would gradually unravel. A poor performance, an unexpected loss, just because the umpire asked him to toss the ball when he served.

My current team-mate Yordan is forever complaining to umpires about opponents' illegal serves. It often creates a bad feeling, but he feels he is entitled to do this. Yordan probably takes it a bit too far sometimes. Even if he has no problem returning an opponent's illegal serve, he will still complain because he knows how much it puts his opponent off his game.

In one league match, Yordan was playing an experienced player who also happened to be a respected Cambridgeshire coach. This player sometimes served legally but sometimes served from the hand, hardly throwing the ball up at all. Yordan complained. There was a frank discussion and Yordan's opponent completely lost the plot. His game went into meltdown. He couldn't use his spinny illegal serves any more and had to use weaker serves. He started throwing the ball very high when serving to prove a point and was frequently lashing out at the ball in frustration. Inevitably, Yordan won the match. This meltdown would have been avoided if the player could consistently serve legally. And the outcome of the match could have been very different.

What's the moral of these stories? If you don't serve legally, you will come unstuck at some point. An opponent will complain or an umpire will enforce the rules. If you haven't developed effective serves with a legal service action, your service game will transform from a strength to a weakness in an instance. Your entire game could suffer as a result.

How to change your illegal service habit

I coach a few players who have illegal serves. They want to serve legally, but struggle to do so. Their serves are illegal, usually because they don't toss the ball. When they try to serve legally, their serves become much weaker. The part they find most difficult is changing the timing of their swing when serving. With their illegal serve, they essentially release the ball and swing straight away.

For a legal serve, you have to toss the ball up and wait for it to come back down again. This is what causes the problem. Some players mistime the swing and miss the ball completely. Other players end up following the toss with their bat and contacting the ball high above the table, resulting in a very bouncy serve. The key is timing. You have to get used to the very different timing when contacting the ball as it goes up and comes back down again.

It can take time to develop legal serves if you have an ingrained illegal service action. But it really is worth putting in the effort to serve legally. If you want extra incentive, I believe you can do much stronger serves when serving legally. When you toss the ball up and contact the ball as it's falling you'll find you can generate more spin, speed, variation and deception. Plus, you'll never be put off your game by an annoying interfering umpire!

Improving your serves

The easiest and quickest way to improve your service game is to develop the serves you already use. Some players get obsessed with learning new serves, hoping to find a killer serve which no one can return. Unfortunately no such serve exists. By always experimenting with new serves, these players never really master any serves.

There are only a few serves you actually need:

- A backspin serve is useful to make it hard for your opponent to attack.
- A topspin serve is useful to set up a fast rally, especially if you like this type of play.
- A sidespin serve with backspin, and a sidespin serve with topspin, are both useful to add some variation and confusion.
- A serve with no spin, or very little spin, is a nice extra option to mess with your opponent.

This is all you need. You can do all these serves with one similar service action. You don't need twenty different types of service action.

I'm sure you already have at least one decent serve. A serve which you feel comfortable using and gives your opponents a bit of trouble.

But how can you make it even better? How can you develop this serve to win more points, win more matches and compete at a higher level? Here's four areas you should focus on:

1. **Service height** – Try to keep your serve as low over the net as possible. The lower the ball travels over the net, the harder it is to attack. You will force your opponent to play more defensively or passively. If your opponent does attack, she will have to spin up more, resulting in a slower attack. If your serve is too bouncy, it is easier for your opponent to hit down on the ball and be very aggressive. To keep the serve low, make sure you contact the ball around net height. If your contact point is too high, the serve will bounce higher.

2. **Ball placement** – Try to serve to different positions on the table with the same service action. As a rough guide, you should focus on six positions. (1) Short backhand (2) Short middle (3) Short forehand (4) Long backhand (5) Long middle (6) Long forehand. If you can hit these six different positions with the same service action, it makes it much harder for your opponent to know what you are going to do. There will always be one position out of these six which your opponent will find tricky.

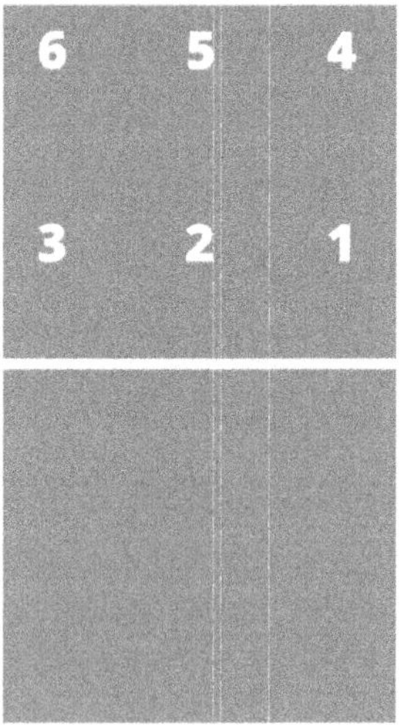

I have often found a long, fast sidespin serve to an opponent's elbow (the crossover area between backhand and forehand) a particularly effective position. If you aim for the elbow, you force your opponent to make a decision. Should she use her forehand or backhand? If there is any indecision or the player does not move, she is likely to play a very awkward stroke, making an error or giving you an easy ball to attack.

To add even more variation, you can do half-long serves. These are serves where the second bounce on the opponent's side is just past the end of the table. Half-long serves are effective because they are not easy to attack strongly, and difficult to return short, giving plenty of opportunities for a third ball attack.

3. **Degree of spin** – How spinny are your serves? Could you generate more spin? Even 10% extra? 5% extra? 1% extra? It all counts. The more spin you can generate, the more problems you will cause. We sometimes take our best serves for granted. We think they are complete, but there is usually more we can get out of them. To generate more spin you need a relaxed wrist and a whipping motion, brushing the ball with plenty of bat acceleration. How much more can you get out of your best serve?

Being able to serve with maximum spin has another significant benefit. It allows more scope to vary the degree of spin. You could serve with very heavy spin. You could serve with medium spin. You could serve with no spin. All three will need to be returned in a slightly different way by your opponent. Your opponent has to work harder.

I like to start with two or three heavy spin serves. I want to give my opponent something to fear. But as a match progresses I will vary the degree of spin. See how my opponent responds to some lighter spin or no spin. In the best-case scenario, my opponent will struggle to read the degree of spin and lose all confidence. If this happens, I know I am going to win many points when I serve.

4. **Spin variation** - Can you do different spin variations with broadly the same service action, i.e. backspin, side-backspin, topspin, side-topspin, no spin? This can give you a big advantage, as your opponent has to work much harder to read the spin.

My favourite service action is the forehand pendulum. I stand on the backhand side of the table, sideways on. With this action I can generate backspin, side-backspin, topspin, side-topspin, no spin. The backswing is always the same, but just at the point of contact, I can adjust my bat angle and swing trajectory to create different spins. If my opponent is not observing closely, I can win many cheap points.

Have a think about your best serve. Can you do different spin variations? If yes, well done. You most probably have a strong service game. If no, think about how you can include the missing spin variations in your action. How will you need to change your bat angle, contact point and swing trajectory?

Service options

If you work on these areas - ball placement, degree of spin and spin variation - you can transform an existing serve. Let's say you have a service action with only one variation, e.g...

- backspin
- short to middle

If you apply ball placement, degree of spin and spin variation, you can transform this serve into a serve with multiple variations…

- backspin, side-backspin or no spin
- short, half-long, long
- wide backhand, wide forehand, middle

That's a lot of different options. This helps massively in a match, as it's much harder for your opponent to get used to your serve. You'll often find that different opponents will struggle against different variations. One opponent may find the short backspin serve to the backhand easy to deal with, but struggle with a short backspin serve to the forehand. The next opponent may find all short backspin serves easy to deal with, but struggle with long backspin serves. The next opponent might find all backspin serves easy to deal with, but will misread when you serve with no-spin. Your job is to find out which variation is going to be effective against which opponent.

If you only have one variation of the serve, and your opponent returns it easily, you're a bit stuck. You may have to stop using the serve. But if you keep changing the length, placement and spin, there is more chance of finding a variation of the serve which gives your opponent difficulty. See what you can do with your favourite serve. You will most likely get a much quicker and bigger benefit by improving a serve you are already familiar with, than trying to learn something completely new.

Solo service practice

One of the best ways to improve your table tennis serves is solo practice. You get a box of balls and serve, serve, serve. I admit, this can be pretty boring. You need plenty of motivation to do this regularly. But if you can find the time and mental energy for some solo service practice, you can improve your serves a lot.

In 2015, I attended the Werner Schlager Academy in Austria. This was a club for professional players to train. I was in the amateur group, but I got to observe the training methods of the professional players. I was struck by how many of them did solo service practice. Before their main training session, they would spend 30-60 minutes just serving and serving. Nothing else, just serves. They used this dedicated service practice time to perfect their existing serves and try out new things.

You do need to be fairly committed to spend this amount of time practising serves on a regular basis, but it really can make a difference. If you do have the inclination to do some solo service practice, here are three tips to help you.

1. **Only use one ball at a time** - The temptation is to have three or four balls in your hand, so you don't have to keep picking up a new ball for each serve. But when you hold a few balls in your hand, the toss will be slightly different compared to if you have one ball. In a match, you have one ball in your hand. You want your service practice to replicate a

real match as closely as possible. Serve with only one ball in your hand. The toss will then be the same as when you serve in a match.

2. **Complete the service action** - It's easy to get into a rhythm of serve, pick up a new ball, serve, pick up a new ball and not complete the full service action (I am guilty of doing this). Instead, you should serve, recover to your ready position, as though you had an opponent to return the ball. This is the full service action. You can even shadow play the third ball if you want to. In a match you wouldn't serve and just stop, so you shouldn't in solo service practice either. Serve, recover to your ready position and shadow play third ball (optional).

3. **Serve at the same tempo as you would during a match** - If you have rituals before you serve in a match, do the same during solo practice. If you take your time whilst serving during a match, do the same during solo practice. If you serve quickly during matches to unsettle your opponent, do the same during solo practice. You get the idea. Try to keep the tempo of your solo service practice the same as matches. The closer you can replicate a match situation, the more beneficial your solo practice will be.

Improving the quality of your serves

The main purpose of solo service practice is to improve the quality of your serves. You should focus on the following areas:

- Better placement – Serve to different positions on the table and different lengths.
- Extra spin – Try to increase your racket speed, whilst brushing the ball, to generate more spin.
- Variation – Try to keep the same service action, but vary the contact to produce spin variation.
- Serve height – Keep your serves as low over the net as you can.
- Consistency – When you try new things - like any of the above - you will make mistakes to begin with. Ultimately, you are aiming for high consistency. You want good quality serves, which you can execute again and again.

You don't necessarily have to focus on all these things at the same time during solo service practice. You can just focus on one or two elements at a time, to maximise the learning process. You might just focus on getting extra spin in your first session. Then in the next session, you might focus on getting extra spin and improving the placement. Then in the next session, your focus might be on spin variation. The choice is yours.

How often should you practise your serves?

Any time you can make for solo service practice is better than none. The longer you spend practising your serves (e.g. 30-60 minutes), the more you'll improve. But I am realistic. You probably do not have this much time to dedicate to solo service practice. Work, family and other commitments take up most of your time. Any time you do have for table tennis, you probably just want to play, rather than practise serves. I understand this because I feel the same way. But if you can find *some* time for some solo service practice, you will improve your serves. Just a few minutes a week can make a difference.

The number of serves you practise really depends on how long your session is. If you only have a short amount of time (5-10 minutes), just focus on one or two serves. If you have a longer amount of time, then you can focus on more serves. You should avoid doing loads of different serves in a short period of time, as you won't improve anything. You'll get the biggest improvement by focusing on fewer serves, but doing them really well.

Serves can get better if you practise, but they can also get worse if you never practise. Even if your serves get really good, it doesn't mean you should stop practising. You might not need to practise quite as much as before (when you were developing your serves to get to a high standard), but you need to keep on practising to keep them at a high standard.

The perfect serve

What is the best table tennis serve you can do? A serve which is unreadable? A serve which is unreturnable? A serve which is guaranteed to win you a point against any opponent? I'm going to disappoint you. There is no single unreadable and unreturnable table tennis serve, which will beat all opponents. Every serve is returnable if you know how.

However, it is possible to execute the perfect table tennis serve, against the right opponent at the right time in a match. Let me explain what I mean. Think of a serve you do. Your favourite serve. Now look at the diagram.

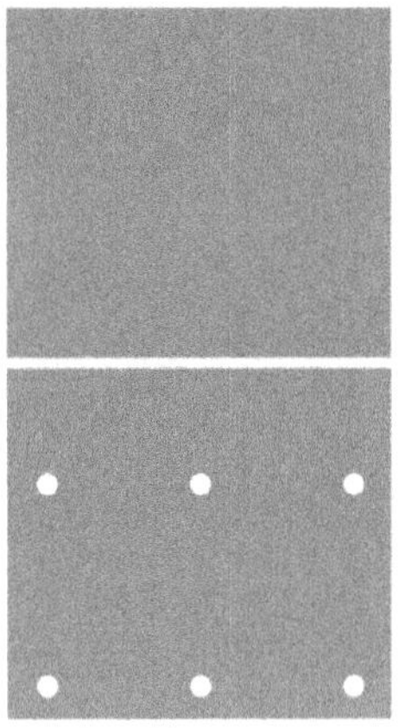

The table has six positions where you can place your serve. Three long and three short. I have already discussed the importance of being able to serve to different positions earlier in the chapter. Why is this so important? It's unlikely your opponent will be able to return the ball equally well from each position. Your opponent may be able to return your favourite serve brilliantly if it is aimed long to her backhand. But the same opponent may struggle with the same serve if it is served short to her forehand. Even if you face a much stronger opponent, there will usually be a position on the table where she is weaker. Your job is to find out where that weak position is. How do you do this? There are two main ways.

1. **Observation**. When you're at a tournament or a league match and waiting to play, don't sit idly staring into space or mess around with your phone. Use the opportunity to observe your opponents. Try to identify which types of serve they struggle with and where the serves are placed. This will give you a head start before your match has even begun.

2. **Trial and error**. When you play an opponent for the first time, you need to try out your serve to different positions. You need to quickly establish her strong areas and weak areas. The first game of the match is an ideal time to do this. If you can work out early your opponent's weak area, you have the rest of the match to exploit it. If you don't test different areas until you're behind and close to defeat, it will most likely be too late. The more you play the same opponent, the more you will build up a knowledge of the best positions you should serve to and less trial and error will be needed.

Using your serve strategically

Your main goal when targeting your opponent's weak area, is to get a weak return of serve. This does not necessarily mean a miss (although this is a bonus). A weak return also means a loose ball – something which is returned a little high and is easy to attack. A weak return can also be a predictable return. The return of serve may actually be decent, but if it is predictable, you can prepare for, and execute, a strong third ball attack.

When you have identified your opponent's weak position, you need to think about using your serve strategically. You should avoid using the same serve to the same position all the time, as your opponent may start getting used to it. But you don't want to use the serve too infrequently either. You need to take advantage of the weakness. Think about using the serve at key points in the match. These are:

1. **At the beginning of a game**. It's great to build an early lead. You put your opponent under pressure straight away. You create some breathing space, which will help you to relax and hopefully extend your lead even further.

2. **In the middle of the game**. If I'm behind (6-4), two good serves can get me level with my opponent. If tied, (6-6), two good serves can nudge me in the lead and put me within touching distance of a game point. If I'm in the lead (6-4), it can help me build a significant points lead.

3. **At the end of a close game**. This is when your favourite serve aimed at your opponent's weak point can be most effective. When a player has game point or is facing a game point in a close game (i.e. the score is 10-9), she will often play a little more cautiously. She may well return your serve even weaker than before. This is a great opportunity for you to either save a game point (if 9-10) or win the game (if 10-9).

This is what I mean by the perfect serve. You use the right serve, in the right position, at the right time in a match, against the right opponent, and you win the point. Perfect. And the good news? You already have the perfect table tennis serve in your game. You don't need to learn a new wonder serve. Just take your favourite serve and learn to serve it to different positions. When you can serve it to different positions, you can then test out which area is most effective against each opponent. When you have found an opponent's weak area, you can exploit it for lots of easy points.

Long serves

In amateur table tennis, especially at lower levels, you can dominate your opponents with long serves. These are serves which land very deep on your opponent's side of the table, ideally with a lot of speed and spin.

When I started as a coach, I discouraged players from doing too many long serves in a match. I told them it was too risky because long serves are easier to attack. I told them to mainly serve short, or half-long - where the second bounce on the opponent's side is just past the end of the table. These shorter serves are much harder to attack.

I picked up this advice from other top coaches, and I was merely repeating what they had told me. I think this is actually good advice, but only if you are playing at a higher level, against really good attacking players. Over the years, I have come to the conclusion this may not be the best advice for all players, especially lower level players.

If you play at a lower level, I find the opposite is actually true. Lower level opponents tend to be more defensive and passive (lots of pushes, prods, swipes and chops). They are less bothered by short and half-long serves because they are not looking to attack. They mainly want to play safe, which is easier to do when returning shorter serves.

Long serves, however, can give lower level players nightmares. These players have less confidence and consistency when attacking, so they rarely attack long serves. Instead, they still push, prod, swipe and chop, but because the serve is long, fast and spinny it is far harder for them to control the ball. Or if they do attack, the stroke is often wild and erratic.

The result? The ball flies off the rubber high, wide, long or in the net, giving the server either a cheap point or an easy ball to attack. Now when I coach lower level players, I tell them that it is absolutely fine to do lots of long serves. Serving long is often the best tactical approach against other lower level players.

Good quality long serves can also be very effective at high amateur levels too and even at the professional level against some opponents. My team-mate Yordan - the unorthodox player I mentioned in the previous chapter - has a great range of long serves. He uses long backspin serves, long topspin serves and long serves with a mixture of sidespin with backspin and sidespin with topspin. The ball comes fast, deep and loaded with spin. Almost all his serves are long. I have been playing with Yordan for many years and have seen first hand how effective long serves can be. Lower level players don't really stand a chance against his serves, but I have also seen his serves baffle, demoralise and defeat players of a much higher ranking. Against most opponents Yordan's serves will give him a three to six point advantage. This helps him maintain a high win percentage, even though other areas of his game can be inconsistent.

The same is true for me. In some matches I start serving short or half-long, but don't seem to gain much of an advantage. But when I start serving long, fast and spinny, it can be a game changer. If I sense my opponent is really uncomfortable returning the long serves, I serve long much more often and the match dynamics completely change.

What is a good long serve?

If your long serves are too slow or too bouncy or a bit too short, then they can be easy to attack by a player of any standard.

You do need a bit of quality when serving long. A good long serve should:

- be fast
- go low over the net
- bounce close to the end of the table
- be placed in a corner or to a player's elbow
- be disguised (not obvious to your opponent that you're about to do it)

In terms of spin, a good long serve could be topspin, side-top, side-back, backspin, or no spin. If you can develop a range of long serves with different spins, like my team-mate Yordan has, you can cause havoc.

The key to executing a fast long serve is to get the first bounce (on your side), close to your end of the table. This means the ball will have enough space to clear the net and come back down on the other side. If your first bounce is too close to the net, it will usually end up in the net. And the second bounce should be close to your opponent's end of the table.

I strongly believe every player should develop at least one very good long serve - a serve which is fast and spinny. Of course, it's important to practise short and half-long serves too, but don't neglect long serves. At lower levels, you can win a lot of cheap points with long serves. At higher levels, using a few more long serves can be a great way to keep your opponent guessing and unsettled.

Always expect your serve to be returned

If you have good serves, it can be very tempting to serve and hope your opponent makes a mistake. Serve. Miss. Point to me! It's a great feeling. But serving with the expectation, or hope, that your opponent will miss can develop into a bad habit. The habit being that you don't recover properly after your serve. You don't gain an understanding of how your serve is likely to be returned and what shot you should play next.

If you serve with the expectation that the ball won't be returned, guess what happens? You ball-watch. You wait to see how your opponent deals with the serve, hoping she will make an error. When the ball is returned, you're taken by surprise. You're not prepared for the third ball. You then play a weak shot and pass the advantage to your opponent.

No matter how good your serves are, it's important to get into the habit of always expecting your serve to be returned. Not only should you expect your serve to be returned, you also need to think about how your serve is likely to be returned.

For example, if you serve cross-court to your opponent's backhand, 80-90% of the time the ball will be returned cross-court to your backhand. If you serve to the middle, the ball is more likely to be returned to a more central position. If you serve really short, you may well get a short return. If you serve long and fast, you're almost guaranteed to get a long return.

And what about spin? If you serve backspin, more often than not it will be returned as backspin. If you serve topspin, more often than not it will be returned as topspin. If you serve sidespin (ball spinning clockwise) the ball will more likely kick back to your backhand. If you serve sidespin (ball spinning counter-clockwise), the ball will more likely kick back to your forehand.

With this knowledge you can prepare much better for the third ball. Against a more defensive player, if you do a backspin serve cross-court to her backhand, there is a good chance she will return the ball with backspin to your backhand. Therefore, you can prepare to play a backhand loop third ball attack. Against a more attacking player, there is a greater chance she will loop your backspin serve, so you should also be prepared to play a block or counter-topspin.

I am slightly simplifying things here. You can't guarantee with absolute certainty how your serve will be returned. Your opponent may have other ideas and return your serve in a way you weren't anticipating. But most players are fairly predictable (myself included!) and will only return each of your serves in one or two ways. Therefore, you can make reasonable assumptions, based upon the playing style and strengths and weaknesses of your opponent, about how the ball is likely to be returned.

With every serve you do, think about your spin, speed and placement and anticipate where the ball may be returned. You can then prepare for the third ball, rather than be taken by surprise when the ball is returned. If your opponent *does* make a mistake from your serve – either by putting the ball into the net or hitting it long – well that's a bonus. But the important thing is that you were prepared for the ball to be returned.

This really elevates your service game to the next level. Some players won't be able to return your strong serves. Great. Other players will. But if you understand how your serves are likely to be returned, and if you can take advantage of any predictable returns with strong third ball attacks, then you can keep your opponent on the back foot. You have the early advantage in the rally. You initiate the first attack. You are the player most likely to win the point.

Service tactics to win cheap points

Let's finish this chapter with some serves I use to win cheap points. First, a warning. Some of these serves will work brilliantly against one opponent, but may be totally ineffective against another opponent. Your job is to find out which serves work against which opponent, and which serves do not. And as I have just explained, it's not all about trying to win the point directly from the serve (although this is a bonus). It's just as much about getting your opponent to return the ball in a predictable way, so you can take control of the rally. Let's look at some of my favourite service tactics to win cheap points.

Fast sidespin to the hip

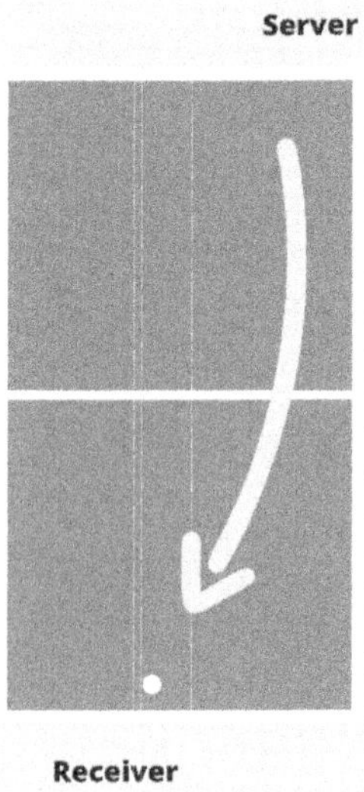

What to do:

- Serve from the backhand corner
- Serve fast and long with sidespin
- Aim to get the ball to swing into your opponent's hip

The purpose of this serve is to target your opponent's crossover position, i.e. her right hip if she is a right-handed player. This is the small area where your opponent has to decide whether to play backhand or forehand. If you serve at speed, your opponent has less time to make this decision and move her feet. The result? If the player doesn't move, she has no space to play a stroke and will often make an error or make a weak return for you to attack. The crossover position is quite a small target area. If your serve drifts too much to the centre of the body, your opponent will be able to return with her backhand. If the ball doesn't turn enough, your opponent will be able to return with her forehand. You have to find the small space in between her forehand and backhand, i.e. her hip. Keep hitting this target and you will win lots of points.

Very wide sidespin

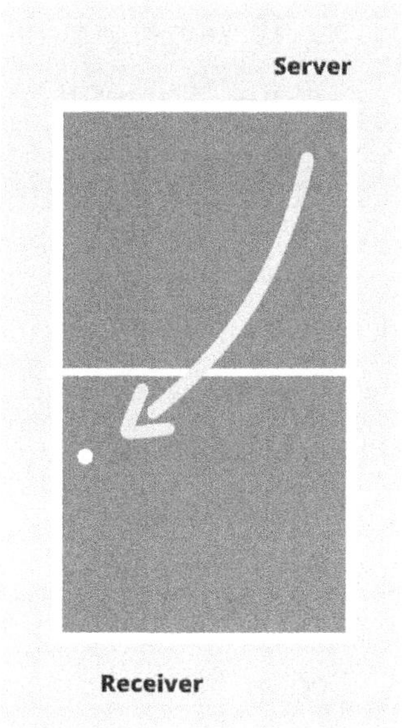

What to do:

- Serve from the backhand corner
- Serve very wide to your opponent's backhand with sidespin
- Stay in the backhand corner. When the ball is returned, play a quick attack to the opposite corner

This is a good serve to use if an opponent's footwork is poor. The aim is to serve very wide, so the ball keeps moving off the side of the table. This will move your opponent out wide to his backhand side, leaving the table wide open for an easy third ball attack.

If your opponent doesn't move well, he may never reach the serve. You'll ace him. If he does get to it, 90% of the time he will be so surprised he will just return the ball where it came from. Just stay in the backhand corner and play a quick shot to the open side of the table.

Long, heavy backspin

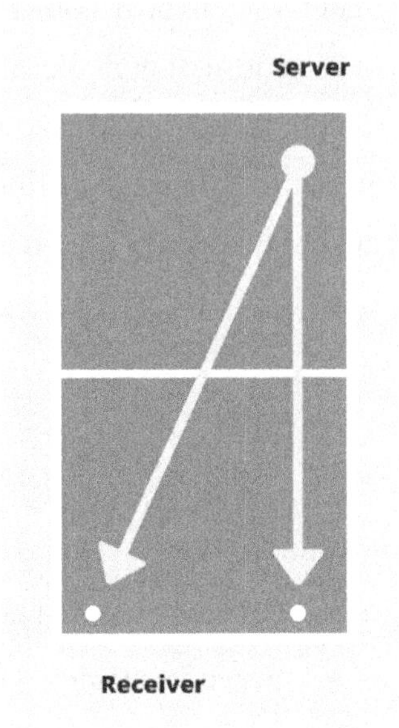

What to do:

- Serve from the backhand corner
- Serve long, heavy backspin – the ball should bounce close to the end of the table
- If your opponent cannot loop, she will push the serve back
- Now you can loop the third ball

At local league level, especially in lower divisions, players struggle to attack long heavy backspin serves. They don't have good enough looping technique. Rather than attack, your opponent may just push the ball back. If she prefers to push, rather than loop, you can use this serve to set up a predictable return every single time. Long backspin serve = push return. Another long backspin serve = another push return.

Because the backspin serve is long, her push will come deep, which will give you a good opportunity to loop the third ball. If you want to set up your backhand loop, serve cross-court. If you want to set up a forehand loop, serve more to the middle or forehand side.

Topspin to the weak side

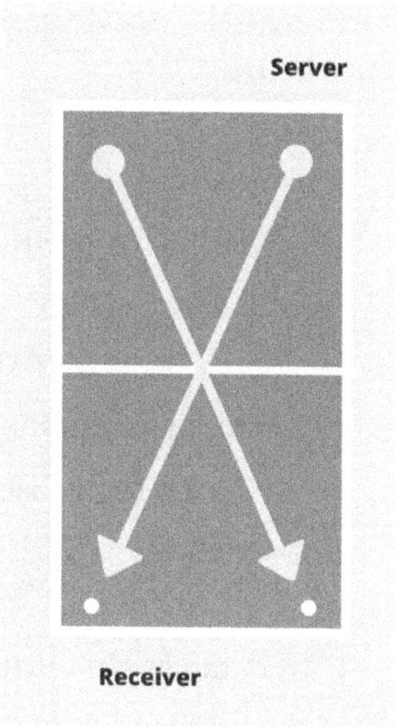

What to do:

- Serve from any position
- Serve topspin long to your opponent's weaker side
- Get ready for a passive return, and then you topspin, or drive, the third ball

Topspin serves are often underrated and underused. I think this is because they are not particularly difficult to return and if a player has a strong attack, he may wallop the ball past you. However, the real advantage of a topspin serve is that the return is very predictable. You serve topspin, 95% of the time your opponent will return with topspin. The key is to target your opponent's weaker side, if he has one. If a player has a weak backhand, a long topspin serve should cause him all kinds of problems. He may passively prod at the ball, causing it to pop up high, and you then have a great opportunity to attack the third ball. Even if he returns the serve more confidently – no problem – it will just be topspin and you will be ready and waiting to attack anyway.

Backhand sidespin from the forehand corner

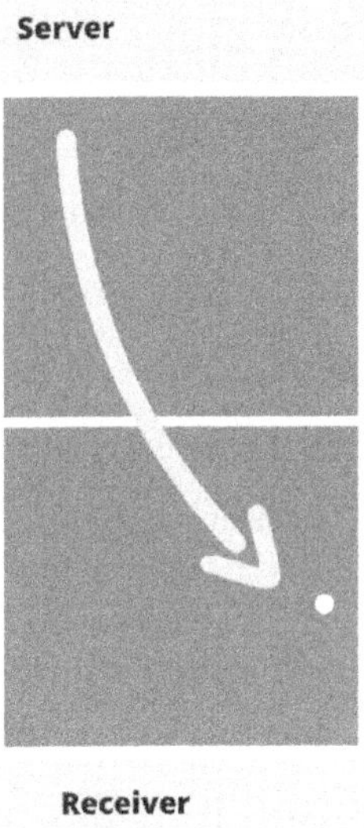

What to do:

- Serve with your backhand from the forehand corner
- Serve wide with sidespin so it cuts across your opponent's forehand
- Prepare for a backhand third ball attack

Players rarely serve with their backhand from the forehand corner. It doesn't make that much sense, as you take your forehand out of the game and you leave your own backhand corner very exposed. However, if you have a strong backhand attack, this serve can really work for you. The serve itself can cause loads of problems, as the sidespin cuts right across an opponent's forehand, much like a left-handed player serving to a right-handed player. Players just aren't used to serves coming from this angle. If they're not used to it, they will make plenty of mistakes. If the ball is returned, it is usually returned cross-court, straight into the server's backhand attacking zone. Then boom! Point over.

Bouncy backspin

I'll finish with something fun to try. I often noticed that when my serve went horribly wrong and bounced up high, my opponent would be so surprised he would completely mess up the return of serve. I would apologise for winning the point by doing such a rubbish serve, and my opponent would just look embarrassed. Now I do it on purpose, usually when I have a comfortable lead. I throw in a bouncy backspin serve and watch in amazement as the change in trajectory and speed completely panics an opponent. I have found that bouncy backspin works best because players underestimate how much backspin is on the ball, and they don't loop it enough to lift it over the net. This doesn't work against everyone. Some players blast the ball past me, making me look silly. But it's something fun to experiment with.

~

That's some of my sneaky service tactics. It's not a complete list. I have many others, but I need to keep some secret in case I ever play you! The serves which work for me, might also work for you or they might not. Experiment and see how you get on. But try to develop your own sneaky service tactics. It's useful to have a few tricks up your sleeve to win some cheap points.

Returning serves

Returning serves is hard. It's the aspect of table tennis most players at the beginner and intermediate levels struggle with the most. It's easy to understand why. There's a lot of different spin, speed and placement variations your opponent can use when serving. Plus all the different service actions – some short and sharp, others with big exaggerated swings. So much variation. So much uncertainty. So little time to react. Returning serves can be very daunting.

I find it hard too. It's an area of the game where I still lose too many points. It can be very frustrating. You feel you are better than your opponent in most aspects of the match, but you keep messing up the return of serve. The match is then much closer than it should be - or you actually lose - because you can't return those damn serves.

Returning serves is just as important as your own service game. But unlike your own serves, you are not in control. You have to react to what your opponent is doing. This requires a different set of skills.

Over the years I have worked hard to improve my ability to return serves. It has been a big weakness, so I have given it extra attention. So many times in training sessions, I have asked my training partner to just serve at me, again and again. I have tried different approaches. Some have worked better than others. I'm still trying to find exactly the right approach for my game, but I have made significant improvement.

In this chapter, I will explain how you can return more serves - how to read spin, how to get more balls back on the table and how to put your opponent under pressure. I will remove the fear factor when returning serves, increase your confidence and hopefully transform your ability to return serves into a strength.

Reading service spin

To return serves well, you need to read the spin. It sounds obvious, doesn't it? But you'd be amazed how many players don't really focus on reading the spin of the serve. If you have no idea what the spin is, then you have to guess. You might guess right. You might guess wrong. Either way it will be a guess, and guessing doesn't usually end well.

So, reading service spin is essential. How do you do this? The first step, and the most important step, is watching your opponent, like a hawk. More specifically, you need to watch your opponent's bat. Even more specifically, you need to watch your opponent's bat as it contacts the ball. This is the key moment. This is where you have the earliest possible clue as to the spin on the ball. It's this fraction of a second which gives you the maximum amount of time to react. Blink and you'll miss it. You need to maintain an intense focus on the player on the other side of the table. If your opponent's bat is moving down as it contacts the ball, then the serve will be backspin. If the bat is moving up as it contacts the ball, then the serve will be topspin. A simple approach, but surprisingly effective. Bat down = backspin. Bat up = topspin.

With some opponents, the service spin is very obvious. There is no tricky service action. No attempt at disguise. Just a straightforward backspin or topspin motion. By watching the server closely, you can easily pick out what the spin is. With better players, it can be harder. The up or down movement may be very subtle. There may be a lot of distraction with an exaggerated service motion. Or there might be some clever deception to confuse you. Even though it is harder, by watching very closely you can still pick out the up or down movement when the server contacts the ball. If you don't watch, you have no chance.

The secondary visual clue is observing how the ball moves. In general, backspin serves will have a lower bounce, stay lower over the net and slow down. Topspin serves will have a higher bounce, jump up more over the net and kick towards you. It is risky to attempt to read the spin on the ball bounce alone. You give yourself very little time to react. By the time the ball bounces for the first time and moves over the net, it is almost upon you. Your decision-making has been reduced to a fraction of a fraction of a second.

Watching the server's initial contact with the ball gives you the most amount of time to react. Watching how the ball moves gives you additional information. Put the two together and you should have a decent idea of what spin is on the ball.

Sidespin serves

How about sidespin serves? These cause a lot of problems. Some players tend to panic when they receive a sidespin serve and tentatively prod at the ball, sending it wide off the table. So, what is the best way to return sidespin serves? I don't actually treat sidespin as a separate category of serve. Why is this? Well, many serves will have an element of sidespin, but it is sidespin with *something*. It will either be sidespin with backspin or sidespin with topspin. It's rarely the sidespin part of the serve which catches a player out. It is usually that they have misread the backspin or topspin part. For example, I often serve sidespin with topspin. If the player misreads and pushes the ball, the return will be high and easy for me to attack. I also often serve sidespin with backspin. If the player misreads and drives the ball, the return will go into the net. The player has not misread the sidespin. The player has misread the backspin and topspin. The sidespin motion just adds in some extra deception and confusion.

If the bat moves sideways and down, then it will be sidespin with backspin. If the bat moves sideways and up, it will be sidespin with topspin. You just need to focus again on whether the bat is moving up or down on contact with the ball. Keep it simple. Reduce how much information your brain needs to process. You can return these side-topspin and side-backspin serves in the same way you would return a backspin or topspin serve. You will need to make a small adjustment to account for the sidespin, by aiming the ball into a different part of the table. If in doubt, just aim for the middle of the table and the ball will land somewhere, even if there is a lot of sidespin.

Reading the degree of spin

To progress even more, you need to be able to read the degree of spin. This is definitely a more advanced skill, but something you should aspire to. A backspin serve could be heavy backspin or light backspin. A topspin serve could be heavy topspin or light topspin. A serve could have very little spin at all, something we call a no spin serve or a float serve.

Watching the bat is once again vital. As well as looking for the up and down motion, you also need to judge the bat speed. A very fast bat and a whipping motion when the server contacts the ball will result in more spin. A slow bat with a more fixed wrist will result in less spin. If you watch the ball very closely, you can see how much it is rotating. Every ball has a brand label on it. If the label is a blur and you can hardly see it, then the ball has lots of spin. If the label is more visible, there will be less spin.

Expand your service knowledge bank

Reading spin is hard, but it is reassuring to know that you can improve significantly with practice. Certainly, from my experience, the longer you play - the more you focus on reading spin - the easier it becomes. I recommend making reading spin and returning serves a regular part of your practice sessions. You can do specific receiving practice, where your partner serves again and again and you return the serves. Make sure the serves are random, so you really have to focus on reading spin. Or if you are doing drills focusing on a different skill, e.g. footwork, you can still start the drill with a return of serve, rather than just putting the ball into play. The more you are exposed to serves, the quicker your skills will develop.

Practise with different players. Seek out players with tricky serves. By doing this you will gradually build up a mental knowledge bank of different types of serves. Over time, you will see less completely new serves. All serves will become more familiar and more comfortable to deal with. Reading spin will become much easier.

Shot selection

You have read the service spin. Now you have to decide which shot to play. Should you flick? Should you touch? Should you push? Should you block? Should you loop? Should you chop? Should you try an outlandish power topspin-drive and watch the server crumple in a heap of despair? There are many options to returning serves. Too many! In this section, I am going to advocate a simplified approach to returning serves. By reducing our options, we can increase our consistency. Make sense? Not yet? OK, let me explain my logic.

In the table below I have listed the different ways you can return eight categories of serves. I have excluded sidespin serves, as I don't treat these as a different type of serve. It will either be sidespin with backspin or sidespin with topspin. A sidespin serve can be returned with the same shots as you would return a backspin or topspin serve, but aiming the ball to a different part of the table to account for the sidespin.

Serve	**Options to return serve**
Short backspin to backhand	Touch / Push / Flick
Short backspin to forehand	Touch / Push / Flick
Short topspin to backhand	Block / Flick / Punch
Short topspin to forehand	Block / Flick / Punch

Long backspin to backhand	Push / Chop / Loop
Long backspin to forehand	Push / Chop /Loop
Long topspin to backhand	Block / Chop /Drive / Topspin
Long topspin to forehand	Block / Chop / Drive / Topspin

We have many options available to return these serves. I have listed nine different strokes, but really our options are much greater. If we break the list down into backhand and forehand strokes, then we have 18 different strokes we could use. If we also consider that we could return balls to our backhand using our forehand or balls to our forehand using our backhand (e.g. the backhand flick), then the options become greater still. And if you factor in all the different variations of flicks, loops, pushes etc, then we have a mind-boggling number of options.

Are you feeling overwhelmed? I know I am. I'm already dealing with the challenge of reading the spin. Now I have to sort through all these options and choose the best one for any given scenario. All in a fraction of a second. Argh! My head is going to explode. Or more likely, with all these options, I'm going to freeze and not do anything at all, other than a passive prod at the ball and mess up the return. We need a different approach. We are going to reduce our decision-making and use fewer options. We are going to keep it simple.

Push and block

The easiest approach is 'push and block'. This is where you return all serves using either a push shot or a block shot. This approach is ideal for beginner and intermediate players, but can also be used at an advanced level for some playing styles. Let's review our table of serves, but this time with our simplified approach:

Serve	**Options to return serve**
Short backspin to backhand	Push
Short backspin to forehand	Push
Short topspin to backhand	Block
Short topspin to forehand	Block
Long backspin to backhand	Push
Long backspin to forehand	Push
Long topspin to backhand	Block
Long topspin to forehand	Block

I have now reduced our options from nine strokes to two strokes. Adding in forehand and backhand and other variations, the total number of strokes has been reduced from 20, to just four - backhand push, forehand push, backhand block and forehand block. All serves can be returned with one of these four strokes.

This is much easier. There is a lot less to think about. I know what strokes I am going to play, either a push or a block. I don't have to worry about all the other options. Should I loop? Should I flick? Should I chop? Should I step around the backhand corner and hit an inside-out forehand cross-court with some fading sidespin? No, I am going to push or block.

As there are fewer options, I have less indecision. I can give more attention to reading the spin and asserting pressure on my opponent.

This is the 'safe' approach. You won't hit too many winners by just pushing and blocking, but you will get many more balls on the table. You will make your opponent play another shot. This in itself will lead to a few more points over the course of a match. If you are good at pushing and blocking, you can actually use these shots to assert quite a bit of pressure. So, it is more than just a 'safe' approach. With aggressive pushes and well-placed blocks you can force errors or weak returns.

Topspin everything

Another simplified approach to returning serves is to be very offensive. You return all serves with an attacking stroke. Basically, topspin everything. This approach is best suited for more advanced players who are very comfortable with a range of attacking shots.

Let's review our table of serves once more:

Serve	**Options to return serve**
Short backspin to backhand	Flick
Short backspin to forehand	Flick
Short topspin to backhand	Flick
Short topspin to forehand	Flick
Long backspin to backhand	Loop
Long backspin to forehand	Loop

Long topspin to backhand	Drive
Long topspin to forehand	Drive

I have listed six strokes - forehand flick, backhand flick, forehand loop, backhand loop, forehand drive and backhand drive. The number of strokes is a little more than 'push and block', but still quite a lot less than our original table.

Once again, all serves can be returned using one of these options. And once again, I have reduced my options. I am going to approach the table with a positive mindset. If serves are short, I will flick. If serves are long, I'm either going to loop or drive. No uncertainty. I am going to attack my opponent's serves and dominate the rally.

This approach is higher risk. You are playing offensive shots, and your margin for error is smaller, but you are far more likely to win points directly from the return of serve. You can really put your opponent on the back foot. Even if you make some unforced errors, it may be worth it if you dominate many of the other points.

Which approach is best?

I have tried both approaches extensively. I actually find the 'push and block' method easier. I have full confidence in my pushing and blocking technique and can adjust my strokes easily to counter different degrees of spin. Both a push and a block are quite short strokes, so I find I have more time to position myself and react. My footwork isn't great, but I can get away with smaller movements when I push and block. I make fewer unforced errors when I return serves in this way. This method also suits my style of play. By pushing and blocking I am inviting my opponent to attack first, but I don't mind this. I have a strong blocking game. It will need to be a very good attack to get through me. If my opponent's shot is not strong, then I can counter attack. I like this approach, as I can get more balls back on the table and then work off my opponent's attacks.

I find the 'topspin everything' approach a little harder. I do OK against players with moderate service spin or a player I am familiar with, but I struggle to attack consistently against stronger servers. I don't have full confidence in my forehand flick and backhand loop. I'm not as good at adjusting my backhand flick to different degrees of spin. There are some gaps in my attacking arsenal. Plus the attacking strokes themselves are a little more complex and better footwork is required. For all these reasons, I have mixed results. I have lost matches by making too many attacking errors. It's tricky to win matches when you make five or six errors when returning serves! My commitment is good, but the results are not so good. However, I have played with, and against, other players who use this 'topspin everything' approach very well. My team-mate James tries to attack as many serves as he can. He doesn't blast the ball. He just tries to get a good topspin contact to gain an early advantage in the rally. He is horrible to play against, as he always seems to get the first attack on the table. During the four years I have played with James in the Cambridge league, he has only ever lost two matches.

In truth, either approach can work. It really does depend on your playing style and the strokes you feel comfortable using. More players at lower levels will push and block. More players at advanced level will be more offensive. You can also combine the two approaches. I sometimes start a match with the 'push and block' approach to get a feel for my opponent's serves. If the serves are not that strong, I might switch to a more attacking mode. Or if the 'push and block' approach is not proving effective, then I will take more risks and start attacking.

But the key point is that by reducing your options, you have less to think about. If you have less to think about, it's easier to get more balls back on the table. If all you have to focus on is a push or a block (or flick or loop for the attacking approach), then you can channel your mental energy into reading the spin and putting your opponent under pressure. You approach the table with a plan and with confidence.

I have suggested two simplified approaches which I have used, but you could make up any approach which complements your strengths. Let's say you have a good push and a strong drive, but not a great flick or loop. You may decide to push all backspin serves and drive all topspin serves. Or you might be a defender with awesome chops. You may decide to return all long serves with a chop and all short serves with a push. Any combination could work. Think about how you could reduce your options when returning serves and then experiment. In the best-case scenario, your simplified approach will increase the number of serves you return and the number of points you win.

Asserting pressure

You have read the spin. You have chosen which shot to play. What next? Ideally, you want to do something decent with your shot. Does this mean going for a winner? Hitting the ball so sweetly, that your opponent has no chance to return? Maybe this is a good choice if the serve is very weak, but in general, I would advise against trying to hit too many winners. You don't need to put yourself under this kind of pressure. Remember the server has the advantage. Instead, your focus should be to apply pressure. Look for ways to put your opponent on the back foot. Try to force your opponent into making a weak shot, so you can control the rally.

How do you do this? Let's start with a simple approach to asserting pressure - ball placement. In the diagram, I have shown two positions to aim your return of serve.

Your opponent's backhand corner and your opponent's forehand corner are two very good positions to aim for. Many players at the amateur level do not recover well after serving. By aiming the ball into the corners, you can keep your opponent off-balance. You might not win the point directly from your return of serve, but you will stretch your opponent and increase the chances he will play a weak shot. You put your opponent under pressure.

Now our approach to returning serves looks like this:

- Read the spin, looking for up and down movement
- Push or block / or flick or loop
- Aim for the corners

That's all there is to it. Beautifully simple, but surprisingly effective. I definitely recommend this approach if returning serves is something you find very hard. With this approach you reduce your options significantly, but the outcome is still very positive. You will return more balls and win more points.

If you are comfortable with this basic approach and feel you are capable of more, then there are other options to apply pressure. Let's start with ball placement again. In the diagram I have added more target areas.

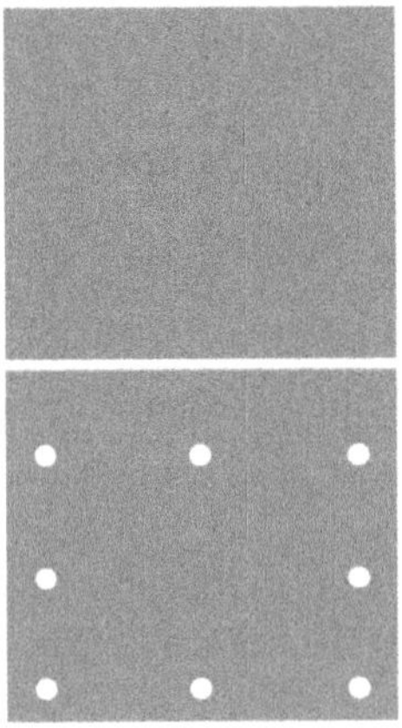

In addition to the corners, I have added the crossover position, wide positions and short positions. Playing to these areas will also put your opponent under pressure, as he will have to move to return your shot.

A short return can make the server lurch forwards. A wide return can make the server reach for the ball. A return to the crossover position can make the server trip over his own feet. The result? You force the server to play a weak shot or make an unforced error. To add even more pressure, you can vary where you return the ball. Sometimes short. Sometimes wide. Sometimes deep into the corner. This unsettles the server. He is never sure where you are going to return the ball. This uncertainty can make the server hesitate, allowing you to dominate the early stage of the rally.

Spin and speed

Spin is another way to assert pressure when returning serves. In particular, heavy spin. If I receive a short backspin serve, my preference is to push. I could push with light backspin, medium backspin or heavy backspin. If I vary how much spin I use, I will create some difficulty for my opponent. But by far the most effective option to apply pressure is to return the serve with heavy backspin. The extra rotation I put on the ball can cause all kinds of problems for my opponent. The ball stays low. It is loaded with backspin. It is intimidating. If my opponent likes to attack, then a heavy backspin push is really going to test his skills. He will have to work much harder to get a decent attack on the table. If my opponent's attacking game is inconsistent, then he will struggle with a heavy backspin push. He will still try to attack, but he is likely to hit the ball into the net. A heavy backspin push with good placement can be a deadly combination.

It's the same with topspin. If you prefer to return a short backspin serve with a backhand flick, you could flick with light topspin, medium topspin or heavy topspin. The option which will assert the most pressure is heavy topspin. This will cause the ball to kick and accelerate at your opponent. You force your opponent back. You are the active player.

Your opponent becomes the passive player. It doesn't have to be a blisteringly fast flick - just extra rotation on the ball - enough to make your opponent feel unsettled. If you combine heavy topspin with good ball placement, your opponent will make errors or weak returns, allowing you to dominate the rally.

A third option to apply pressure is speed. This is where you contact the ball quite early - before it reaches the peak of the bounce - and you also accelerate your shot too. The combination of early timing and a little extra speed takes time away from your opponent. When the server has less time to react, the pressure intensifies. The server finds it much harder to settle after the serve. The ball is already upon him. With less time, the server becomes more passive. The next shot is weaker. Once again, you have the opportunity to dominate.

Ball placement, spin and speed are three excellent options you can use to apply pressure. If you are very comfortable reading spin, and you have mastered most table tennis strokes, then mixing up your return of serves - adding lots of variety - will also create a lot of pressure. However, I don't want to focus on this too much. The theme of this chapter is to keep our approach to returning serves simple. Out of the three options I have given, ball placement is the simplest and the most effective. I suggest making this your priority. Don't go looking for winners. If a serve is very weak, certainly try to punish it. This is fine. But most of the time you are just trying to assert pressure and make life difficult for the server. Force the server to play weak shots. Take away his advantage. If you can do this, then you will have a very effective approach to returning serves.

~

Returning serves is the hardest part of table tennis. There is a temptation to complicate our approach to returning serves more than necessary. Or force our returns too much. Or focus on the latest fancy flick. But getting very good at returning serves involves doing the basics right. Read the spin. Keep your options simple. Put your opponent under pressure. This approach gives you confidence. It gives you a plan of action and allows you to be assertive. You will get more balls on the table and you will win more points.

A quick final word on practice. Whether you choose to follow my advice or ignore it completely (I won't be offended), it is vital that you practise returning serves. In 50% of points you play in matches, you have to return a serve. It is a major part of table tennis and something which many players at amateur level do not take seriously enough. Make returning serves a regular part of your training sessions. Practise with a range of different players to build up your knowledge bank of service motions. Experiment with different approaches - 'push and block', or 'topspin everything', or your own simplified approach. See what works best for you. With regular purposeful practice, your ability to return serves will improve significantly.

Winning points

You serve. Your opponent returns your serve. You are now into the rally. How are you going to win the point?

Some players seem to win points with very little effort. Serve, return, attack - point over. And repeat. Serve, return, attack - point over. How do they make this look so easy? It can be tempting to assume these players win points because they have better technique, or they are just blessed with table tennis 'talent'. But it is important to watch - really watch - how these players actually win points. Where do they put the ball? How much spin? How much speed? How much power? Why is it easy for them?

That's what we are going to explore in this chapter. What options do we have available to win points? How can we make winning points easy for us? I am going to examine five categories - ball placement, spin, speed, power and disruption - considering the merits of each. This will set the scene for the next chapter, where we drill down into specific tactics to win points against different types of players.

Before I turn you into a point winning machine, I'm going to take us on a minor detour. It won't take long, but I think it will be useful to have a quick chat about playing styles.

What is the best playing style to win at table tennis?

One of the great things about table tennis is that there are many ways you can play and win. Some players attack. Some players defend. Others like to mix up defence and attack. Some use lots of spin. Others prefer flat hits. Some players like to stay close to the table. Others will go three metres back. Most players use inverted rubbers, but others use pimples or anti-spin. There are many options, but which is best? Which playing style will help you achieve most success?

All the evidence suggests that some form of attacking playing style will allow you to progress the furthest. This is certainly true of my experience playing local league table tennis. Every time I moved up a division, both in London and Cambridge, I encountered more attacking players. The play would speed up, the spin would increase and opponents would hit the ball harder. In the top division in Cambridge most players have an attacking playing style. Most matches are a battle of attacking strokes. In the levels above my standard, players are even more attacking. At the very pinnacle of the sport - professional table tennis - almost all players have an attacking playing style. Even the defenders aren't truly defensive any more. They attack as much as they defend.

Attacking playing styles tend to dominate. It's easy to understand why. Attackers take the initiative and inject speed and power into the rally. Our court - the table - is small. We play close to each other, only three metres apart. When one player attacks and hits the ball hard and fast, it is difficult for the other player to return the ball. There is very little time to react. The net is also quite low, which makes it easier for an attacker to play direct and fast. If the net was higher, then play would be slower, as players would have to spin up more. All these factors favour the attacking player. It's the most efficient and effective way to win points.

For most players, choosing an attacking playing style is the best option. However, within the category of 'attacker', you have many playing styles to choose from. You could be a:

- Forehand dominated attacker
- Backhand dominated attacker
- Two-wing attacker (forehand and backhand equally strong)

In terms of spin, you could be a:

- Heavy spin attacker
- Topspin drive attacker
- Hitter / puncher

In terms of playing distance, you could be a:

- Close to the table attacker
- Mid-distance attacker
- Far from the table attacker

In terms of equipment, you could use:

- Inverted rubbers on both sides
- Short pimples on one side, inverted rubber on the other side

There are top amateur and professional players, who use any of the combinations above, and probably others that I have not mentioned. Most players prefer to attack with topspin. The modern trend is to be a two-wing attacker - attacking strongly with both forehand and backhand. And players seem to play closer to the table and faster than ever before. But in truth, no one attacking style is better than any other. At amateur level - and the professional level too - you can achieve success with any attacking playing style. If you can master the style of your choice (e.g. forehand dominated, close to the table, flat hits), you can go a long way.

Other playing styles

Whilst some form of attacking playing style is probably best, it is certainly not the only option. In amateur table tennis you can have success with *any* playing style. You might not win many points against a professional player by using lots of pushes or blocks or lobs, but at the amateur level this is very possible. A simple push, a steady block, a half decent chop or a high lob can easily win you a point. The skill level at amateur level is obviously not as high, so it is not essential to attack all the time. This gives amateur players a lot more options when choosing a playing style. Let me introduce you to Roger. He is a veteran of the Cambridge Table Tennis League. He has competed for over 40 years and is still going strong. He wins most of his matches in the second division and wins a few in the top division too. Roger is the complete opposite of the attacking player I have just described. He uses anti-spin rubber on both sides of his bat. He is ultra-defensive. He plays slowly. He will never attack, even if the ball is high. He just keeps putting the ball on the table. He will let his opponent attack and very steadily block and chop the ball back. He is very patient and will keep playing the same defensive shots until his opponent makes a mistake. If Roger plays another defensive player, he doesn't change his approach. He keeps guiding the ball back on the table. Admittedly, Roger's matches against other defensive players are quite painful to watch and have been known to last for quite some time! But Roger doesn't care. He has played the same way all his life and mastered his own unique playing style. And he wins lots of matches. I have lost to Roger on more than one occasion and it is a humbling experience. He is the perfect example that you don't have to be an all-out-attacker to succeed in amateur table tennis.

My playing style is also a bit of a mixture. In some matches I will be more attacking, using flicks, loops and drives to win points. But in other matches I take a more defensive approach, using pushes and blocks to force mistakes. It depends on the level of my opponent and what mood I am in. If I play a weaker opponent, I might opt to use a push and block playing style and only switch to attack mode if I need to. This is not a great habit - a legacy of my inherent cautiousness! But against a weaker opponent, I would back myself to win most matches just by pushing and blocking. I spend a lot of time pushing and blocking when I coach - hours and hours each week feeding other players - so I have got really good at it. When I play more advanced players, my push and block playing style is less effective. Their attacks are stronger, with more speed and spin and better placement. I often become too passive, and push and block too many balls, making it too easy for my opponent to keep on attacking. But even against these stronger players in the top division, I am able to win some matches by mainly using a push and block playing style.

I am not alone. There are three or four very good defenders from other teams who win lots of matches in the top division in Cambridge. I'm quite certain this is replicated across all amateur leagues and tournaments. Attacking players are most common, but there are many others who use alternative playing styles and win lots of matches. At amateur level table tennis there is a huge range of options to choose from. To succeed, you can choose any playing style you want.

As we explore different ways of winning points in this chapter, please keep in mind the advice I share will work with any playing style. I'm not going to encourage you to play a certain way. I want you to work this out for yourself. I want you to embrace your own playing style and develop it. Make it unique to you. But please feel reassured, whatever playing style you use, you have lots of options available to win points and achieve success.

Ball placement

Now that we have established that any playing style can be effective in amateur table tennis, we can look in more detail at the best methods to win points. The first method is ball placement. This is the simplest and quickest way for every player to instantly win more points. You don't need to learn any new shots. You just need to improve where you put the ball. With better ball placement, you can force your opponent to play weak shots or make errors. You also hit a lot more outright winners. But what is good ball placement? Let's look at a few target areas.

Cross-court

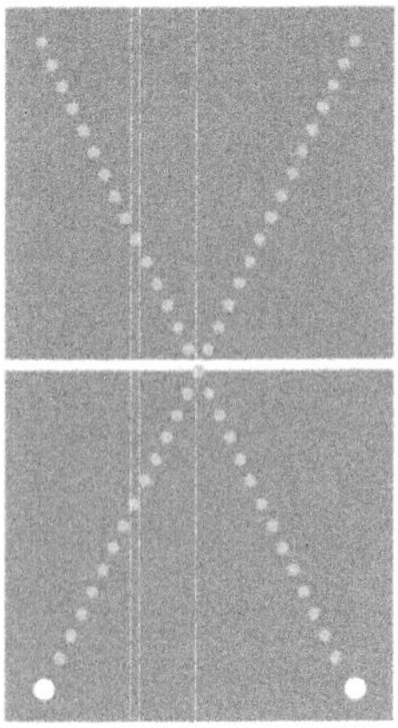

Hitting shots cross-court to the corners is a great place for us to start. Many players use these diagonal shots. It's one of my favourite ball placements too. The diagonal is the longest part of the table, so we have more margin for error and more scope for hitting with power. For maximum effect you really want to aim the ball as much in the corner as you can. If the ball drops short, landing in the middle of the table, it is easier for your opponent to return. But if you hit the corner

- really close to the lines - then your shot will be much harder for your opponent to return.

The depth is very important. Most players at amateur level will either play close to the table or at mid-distance. If the ball lands very deep in the corner, your opponent has little time to react or play a decent stroke. If your opponent is out of position, then you will hit clean winners. Your opponent will watch the ball whizz past. Even if your opponent is a little closer to the ball, a fast attack to the corner can often make your opponent reach out in desperation. Your opponent may get his bat to the ball, but it is unlikely to be a decent shot.

If you are a more defensive player, you can still play pushes and chops deep into the corner from the diagonal. These pushes and chops are hard to attack, as the ball is moving away from your opponent, and the depth gives little time for your opponent to play a full looping stroke. What follows is a rushed, slightly panicked looping shot, which often goes into the bottom of the net.

Down the line

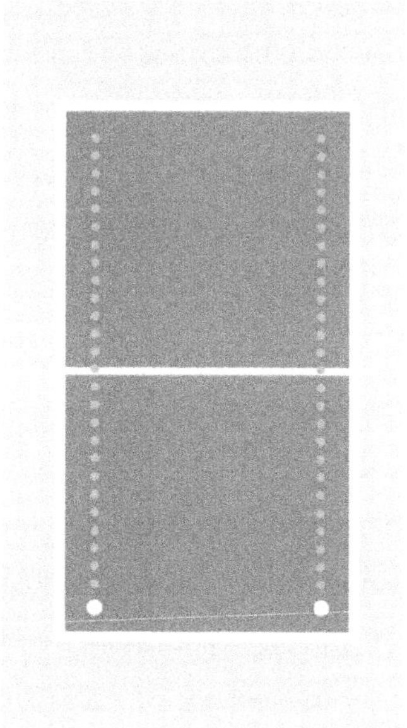

Down the line shots are harder to do. The distance is shorter. The margin for error is a little less. It's difficult to get the same amount of power, compared to playing cross-court. Even though it is harder, if you can play down the line - especially with a little speed - then you can win a lot of points in amateur table tennis.

There are two main reasons why. Firstly, your opponent has less time to react. The distance is shorter, so the ball comes sooner. With less time to react, your opponent has to be very quick to adjust and play a decent shot back. Secondly, players are far less used to dealing with shots down the line. Much of the practice we do is diagonal. Forehand to forehand or backhand to backhand. We are more comfortable dealing with balls which come from this angle. We don't spend anywhere near as much time practising down the line shots. As a result, we tend to be less skilled at dealing with balls coming from this angle. If you start using down the line shots in your matches, you will quickly notice how most opponents struggle to cope.

You need to get the ball close to the side of the table. This is important. The closer to the side of the table, the more your opponent will feel stretched. Even if the ball drops a bit short, if it is close to the side of the table, the shot is likely to be effective. However, if you can get the ball close to the side of the table and deep, i.e. in the corner, then this will maximise the effectiveness. Your opponent has less time to react and less space to play.

A backhand shot down the line can be difficult to read and very effective at putting your opponent under pressure. However, the shot which wins so many points is the forehand down the line. It's easier to hit with more power on the forehand. It targets your opponent's backhand, which is usually the weaker side (presuming you are both using the same hand - right-handed player vs right-handed player or left-handed player vs left-handed player). And players usually expect forehand shots to go cross-court. When you add all this together - a bit of power, less time for your opponent to react, targeting the weaker side and an element of surprise, it becomes clear why a forehand attack down the line is so effective. I have won more direct winners with this shot than any other in my game.

Crossover

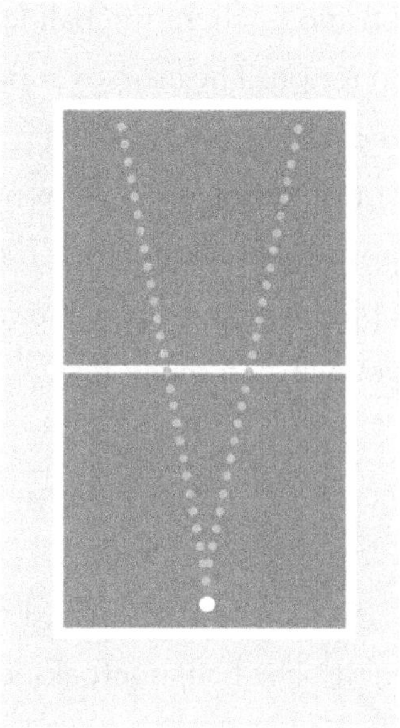

The crossover position is where your opponent transitions from a backhand stroke to a forehand stroke, or vice-versa. It's a small area, located somewhere between an opponent's playing elbow and hip. It is not a fixed position on the table. It will keep moving depending on the position of your opponent.

Shots to the crossover can be very effective as you force your opponent to make a decision. When you play to an opponent's forehand, there is no decision to make. Your opponent will play a forehand. When you play to an opponent's backhand, again there is no decision to make. Your opponent will play a backhand. But when you play to the crossover position, your opponent has to decide whether to return with the forehand or backhand. Your opponent has to move left or right, to get in a good position to return the ball. If your opponent doesn't move, you have a good chance of winning the point. Your opponent will be forced to play an awkward shot or won't be able to return the ball at all.

Ideally, you should target the crossover position with some speed and depth - really get the ball close to the end of the table. This could be an attack or a slightly more assertive defensive shot. If your shot drops short or is too slow, your opponent will have more time to decide what to do. She will be able to move to the left, or to the right, and choose whether to play with the forehand or backhand. A quick shot to the crossover position, where the ball lands near the end of the table is much harder to return. The crossover position is a small target - just that area between the playing elbow and hip. If your shot is outside this area, it is easier for your opponent to the return the ball. But if you can hit the crossover position precisely, then it can be deadly. You take time away from your opponent, and she will have little chance to react. Nine times out of ten, you will win the point.

Wide

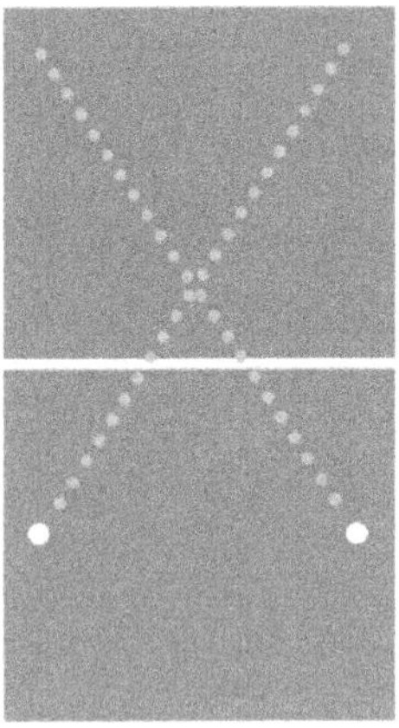

Wide shots are aimed to the side of the table. The ball, if left alone, would continue its direction somewhere between the end of the table and the net, as shown in the diagram. A wide shot could be any type of shot – push, block, flick, topspin, etc – and fast or slow. It's often easier to play a wide shot if the ball is short on either the forehand or backhand side, but you can also play wide shots from behind the table too.

Wide shots are really good at stretching your opponent. If you use width, your opponent has to cover a larger playing area and work harder to stay in the rally. If your opponent has poor footwork, she won't get to your wide shots at all, so it can be a very easy way to win points. If your opponent has OK footwork, you will force her to reach out for your wide shots. If she reaches out for the ball, she will find it harder to maintain balance and play a good quality shot. You often get a weak ball back, which you can attack with your next shot. Even if your opponent has good footwork and can get to your wide shots, you will have succeeded in moving her away from the table, which gives you more space to aim your next shot.

The most basic tactic is to send your opponent wide and then aim your next shot to the opposite side of the table. You move her left and right, chasing down balls. She does all the hard work. You control the rally without breaking sweat. This is a tactic I often use. I don't need a great deal of power when playing these shots. It's the width which causes all the problems. There is something very satisfying about sending an opponent wide, opening up the table and then guiding the ball to the opposite side of the table for a clean winner.

Mix it up

All these ball placement options are effective. Some will work better for your playing style than others. And some options will be more effective against one opponent and less effective against another opponent. You need to experiment and do a little trial and error when you play. If you want to prioritise, I recommend starting with the forehand down the line. This is the shot which can quickly win you extra points.

Really, the best approach is to vary your ball placement. If you always play your shots to the same position, it becomes predictable. Even if the ball placement is good, your opponent will know what to expect and be able to adjust. Instead, play your shots to different areas. Sometimes diagonal to the corners. Sometimes down the line. Sometimes the crossover position. Sometimes wide off the side of the table. Vary the placement and be unpredictable. Your opponent will feel stretched and uncomfortable. You will hit a lot more winners.

Try to get good ball placement with every shot. This means going for a good ball placement when you push. Good ball placement when you topspin. Good ball placement when you block. Good ball placement when you flick. Good ball placement when you smash. Of course, it's not always possible to get every ball into a difficult position for your opponent. Your opponent may be doing the same thing to you and you're simply reacting. But you should aspire to get good ball placement. You should have a mindset of getting good ball placement as often as you can. This will make you much harder to play against.

If ball placement is a new concept for you, you will really need to actively focus on it. I recommend aiming for the lines, with as many balls as possible. At first, you'll probably make mistakes and hit many balls wide or off the end of the table. This is fine. It's what I would call a 'good mistake'. The more you do this, the more accurate you will become and you'll make far fewer mistakes and hit a lot more very good well-placed shots. Eventually, your ball placement skills will become automatic. Your subconscious will take over and you will go for well-placed shots without even thinking about it. Then you will have advanced ball placement skills and will win a lot more points and matches.

Spin, speed and power

Whilst I am a huge fan of ball placement, there are other ways you can win points. We will now turn our attention to three other candidates - spin, speed and power. How can these help us win points? And what works best at amateur level table tennis?

Spin

Table tennis is a game of spin. Every shot we play in table tennis has spin, but from my experience of amateur table tennis it is *heavy* spin which causes the real damage and wins points. Light spin is easy to deal with. Lower level players can handle light spin. Heavy spin is a game changer. Whether a loop, a flick, a lob, a chop or a push, if you really increase the level of spin, you will win extra points.

Heavy spin shots are harder for your opponent to return. It requires a higher level of skill to control heavy spin. Often heavy topspin shots are blocked off the end of the table. Heavy backspin shots are returned into the bottom of the net. At lower levels, the placement doesn't even have to be that good. It's the heavy spin which wins the point.

I'm really putting the emphasis on 'heavy' spin. To generate heavy spin you need to brush the ball with fast racket speed. That's the simplest way of looking at it. How you use your body, how you transfer your weight and how you swing for the ball, will all contribute to the amount of spin you can generate. But don't overcomplicate this. Brush the ball with a fast racket and you can generate heavy spin with many shots - loops, flicks, lobs, pushes and chops.

Think about your game for a moment. How much spin do you generate? Do you often win points where your opponent is unable to return your spin? If yes, congratulations. You play with heavy spin. If you answered no, then you have an opportunity. Pick one or two shots, e.g. a loop or a push, and try to increase the amount of spin you generate. When you apply this in matches, you will start winning points directly from the strength of your spin.

Speed

Our next candidate to win points is speed. For me, this isn't how fast you hit the ball. It's how early you contact the ball. If you play a little closer to the table, use shorter strokes and contact the ball *before* the top of the bounce, you can play with a lot of speed. The early timing is the key. We often talk about contacting the ball at the top of the bounce. This is fine. But if you contact the ball a little earlier - as the ball is rising to the top of the bounce - the effect can be quite significant.

Speed is effective because you take time away from your opponent. The ball is returned sooner. This gives your opponent less time to react. With less time to react, your opponent is rushed to make a decision and play a shot. This is when mistakes happen. A panicked attack or a passive prod and you win the point. If your opponent is out of position, then a quick shot to the open area of the table will often be a winner.

You can play many shots with early timing - drives, flicks, blocks, pushes and counter-topspins. My personal favourite is a block. My opponent hits a big topspin attack. I stay close to the table and with a short stroke and minimal physical energy, I block the ball early - as it is rising. The ball is returned fast. My opponent has little time to recover. The ball whizzes past him for a winner. There is nothing more satisfying.

Think about your game again. Do you contact the ball early? Or do you like to step back and let the ball drop? If you already play with speed, well done. If you are on the slower side, could you add some extra speed into your game? Could you start contacting the ball a little earlier? Try experimenting and see what happens.

Power

Our final candidate is power. This is how hard you can hit the ball. If you hit the ball really hard and it lands on the table, you have a very good chance of winning the point. So, why don't we do this all the time? Well, it's hard to *consistently* hit with lots of power. If you go for big power shots but only manage to get one out of five on the table, then it's not very effective.

Playing with power is good, but you need to find a balance between power and consistency. I like to think about power in percentages. 100% = your maximum power. If you hit your attacks at 100% of your power and you keep missing, just reduce the power of your attacks. Try attacking at 80% of your power rather than 100%. When you take off some of your power, your consistency will increase, sometimes quite considerably. As you're hitting the ball very hard in the first place, you have plenty of scope to reduce the power. A shot at 80% of your power will still be pretty fast and beat most opponents, but it will be much more consistent. You don't have to blast an opponent's head off with your attacks. Just get the ball on the table.

Think about your game again. Do you miss too many power shots? Try reducing the power and see what difference this makes. Or do you rarely win points through hitting the ball hard? If so, you have scope to increase your power. Do this little by little. You don't have to jump from 40% power to 80% power. Instead, nudge yourself up to 50% power. If you are still consistent, nudge yourself up to 60% and so on. Find that percentage where you can play with effective power and still maintain high consistency.

Which option is most effective?

You can win points with all three options - spin, speed and power. These are all tools to add to your game. They work even better when combined with excellent ball placement. At amateur level, I think you can achieve most success with spin and speed. Power is useful - but there is only so much power you actually need to win a point. My team-mate James - the player who has lost only two matches in four league seasons - rarely hits the ball really hard. He doesn't need to. Most of the time he plays with heavy spin and excellent ball placement. This is enough for him to dominate at local league level.

I'm not going to tell you one is better than the other. All three have their merits. The challenge is to see how you can incorporate all three into your game. This doesn't mean you should stay close to the table, take the ball early, play with heavy spin and hit the ball hard. This wouldn't work. You would be a total mess. But let's say you are a player who likes to take the ball late and play with heavy spin. Instead of letting the ball drop, could you play with more speed by using flicks or quick pushes? Or if the ball is a little high, could you try hitting hard, rather than spinning? If you use all three - spin, speed, and power at different times in a match, you can cause mayhem. Your opponent won't know what to do. You will be a point winning machine.

Disruptive shots

Lastly, let's explore shots which disrupt the pace of the game. These are shots which unexpectedly change the speed, spin, length or direction of the ball. Examples of these shots are the chop block, forehand fade, around the net, snake / wiggly, a push with sidespin, a smash with backspin, taking the ball off the bounce, strawberry flick or even a slow and spinny topspin – all sorts of weird and wonderful shots. You can find examples of these if you search on YouTube. Are disruptive shots effective? Will they win you points? Should you use them?

Breaking the rhythm

Players like rhythm. When we train, we like to hit topspin to topspin. The spin stays the same. The bounce is predictable. We feel comfortable. We play well. When we play matches, it's really nice to play against someone who has a consistent rhythm. Win or lose, we know what to expect, and usually play pretty well. Rhythm is nice.

Disruptive shots break this rhythm. A change of pace. A change of timing. A change of spin. A change of direction. A disruptive shot can do all of this at the same time. A great example is a chop block. A normal block will return the ball with topspin. It can still be effective, but your opponent knows what to expect. He recognises the shot and can anticipate the pace, the timing and the spin. By contrast, a chop block changes the spin, the pace and the direction the ball moves. This can be very unsettling. Your opponent now has to adjust - and play a different stroke. The rhythm has been broken. If your opponent is hesitant - he will most likely play a weak shot or make an error. Nice, your point.

Disruptive shots work because they are unusual. The technique is unfamiliar. As well as breaking the rhythm, your opponent may struggle to process the motion of the shot. If your opponent doesn't know what spin is on the ball, it makes it hard to return. There is an element of surprise. When you only have a fraction of a second to make a decision - and you are unsure of the spin - it is very hard to play a good quality shot.

On my YouTube channel, I have made a few videos with Craig Bryant, a former England professional. He has great bat skills and is a master of disruptive shots. During our filming sessions, Craig will mix up traditional shots and disruptive shots. When rallying, sometimes he will hit a blistering - but conventional - forehand topspin past me. Sometimes he will take the pace off the ball and add a lot of sidespin to take me out very wide. Sometimes he will fade his attack in the opposite direction to which his bat is moving. When I attack him, sometimes he will play a conventional block and other times he will throw in a chop block, completely messing with my timing. When returning my serves, sometimes he will flick aggressively to my backhand. Other times he will touch very short or swipe with sidespin or dig deep with heavy backspin. It is horrible to play against. The uncertainty makes me anxious and tight, and I miss shots I would usually get. It is very difficult to process what Craig is doing, when he is using unfamiliar looking strokes. My unconscious mind has no framework to deal with these shots, so I am usually too slow to react and make plenty of errors.

How do you win points?

Let's reflect upon your game. I have discussed five different ways to win points - ball placement, spin, speed, power and disruptive shots. How good are you at each method? Get a piece of paper and make a chart as below. Give yourself a score out of 10 for each method. Award yourself between 8-10 if you win lots of points, 4-7 if you win some points, and 1-3 if you don't win many points.

Method	**Score (10-1)**
Ball placement	8
Spin	5
Speed	8
Power	4
Disruptive shots	1

From my chart you can see that there are two main ways I win points - ball placement and speed. These are my two big strengths, but I have plenty of scope to develop in other areas. I win some points with spin and power, but hardly any with disruptive shots. What should I focus on? Increasing my spin levels is an obvious choice, particularly on my backhand. I rarely beat my opponent with a heavy backhand topspin or loop. I'm more likely to win a point because of the lack of spin! My opponent expects there to be more spin and over compensates. I am also low on the power scale. I'm a little risk averse when I play, but maybe this holds me back. Maybe I need to increase the power and play with a few more risks. There's plenty for me to contemplate.

What does your chart look like? Hopefully, you have scored 8+ for one method. This means you have at least one solid way of winning points. But ideally you need to be 8+ for two methods or more. If you only have one method of reliably winning points, you may become a little predictable. For example, if your super weapon is spin, but your opponent can handle your spin, then you're a bit stuck. Your options to change the dynamics of the game are very limited. However, if you have more than one super weapon, then you can switch strategy. You can play with more speed or power instead. It doesn't matter that your opponent can handle your super spin, as you have other ways of winning points.

If you can score 8+ for three, four or five methods, then you have far more tactical options available. You should have a way of winning points against most opponents. If one method isn't effective, you can switch to another. If that doesn't work, try another. It doesn't guarantee you will win all your matches, but it does increase your chances of winning far more than you lose. You become a more complete and dangerous player.

Which method should you focus on? I passionately believe ball placement is useful for every player. This is essential. Beyond ball placement, there is no right or wrong. It really depends on your preferred playing style. Some players prefer spin, some prefer speed, some prefer power and some like to be completely weird and unconventional. All will win you points. I have competed against - and lost to - players who fit into all these categories.

My challenge to you is this: can you add a new dimension to your game? If you are a spin player, can you develop some power shots to add some variation to your game? If you are a power player, can you add some spinny shots to your game? Mixing up spin and power can make it harder for your opponent to anticipate what you are going to do. Are there one or two disruptive shots you could add to your game? Throwing in an unexpected shot here and there can win you cheap points and feels great when it actually works. I'm not going to dictate what you should do. One of the ongoing themes of this book is for you to think for yourself and come up with your own answers. Take some time to reflect. Where are the gaps in your game? Which methods can you develop to win more points?

Tactics

Let's turn our attention to the person on the other side of the table. Your opponent. One of the toughest challenges in table tennis is learning how to play against - and beat - different styles. Not everyone plays the same. This makes the game harder, but it also makes it a lot more fun in my opinion. Each opponent is a problem you need to solve. What is your opponent's strength? What is your opponent's weakness? What tactics should you use? Play fast? Play slow? Load up with topspin? Keep the game tight with backspin? Play to the backhand? Play to the forehand? There are so many tactical options available to you. How can you find the right ones to use for every opponent you play?

Tactics is a topic I am passionate about. I have played many matches, where I have been technically inferior to my opponent, but tactically more aware. To the casual observer - I am the weaker player. But I have worked out how to apply my strengths to an opponent's weakness and I win the match. If you take two players with the same technical ability, but one player has a much stronger tactical awareness, the player with the tactical strength will win almost every time. Tactics matter.

Tactics is also a huge and very complex topic, with no definite answers. There is a great book by U.S. coach Larry Hodges called *Table Tennis for Thinkers*, which is dedicated to this topic. I highly recommend reading this book if you want to develop a deep understanding of tactics. I have read this book a few times and it has helped me a lot. For my book, I take a simpler approach. In this chapter I share tactics you can use against a wide range of playing styles. For each playing style, I limit myself to three tactics. These are tactics I have used over the past decade and which have worked more often than not. These are not the only tactics which work - definitely not. But I find it easier to focus on a small number of tactics and do them well, rather than having too many possible tactics swirling around my mind, leaving me confused and indecisive. In the heat of a match, I like to keep my options simple and have a clear focus.

The playing styles we will examine include four defensive players (pusher, chopper, blocker and lobber), four attacking players (topspin attacker, mid-distance looper, one-wing attacker and flat hitter) and players who use alternative rubbers (long pimples, short pimples and anti-spin). These are the playing styles you are most likely to encounter in amateur table tennis. The playing styles I refer to are broad categories. The opponents you face might not neatly fit into one category, so you may need to blend tactics from different categories.

My tactical suggestions might work for you. They might not. A lot depends on your own playing style and the options you have available to win points. I encourage you to experiment. Discover for yourself which tactics are effective. Whether it's my tactics which work best, or other tactics which you develop, really doesn't matter. The important thing is that you develop a tactical mindset. As long as you are thinking tactically, then I am happy. So, let's switch our brains to tactical mode and start out-thinking our opponents.

The pusher

Our tactical journey starts with the pusher. This type of player is very common at the lower levels of amateur table tennis. A pusher will happily engage in long, slow, tactical rallies - push, push, push, push, push and push again. If the ball pops up high, the pusher may be tempted to attack, but quite often she will err on the side of caution and push once more. A pusher's aim is to frustrate you. She wants to draw you into a backspin game. She wants to make it hard for you to attack. She wins points through consistency and patience. She will push as many times as necessary, waiting for you to make a pushing error or attempt an attack and miss. A good pusher can be frustrating to play against and difficult to beat.

Tactics to beat a pusher

1. Loop, loop and loop some more - The easiest way to defeat a pusher is by looping. If a push is deep enough (the second bounce is off the end of the table), you should try to play a topspin attack, or a 'loop', as it is often called. This is where you brush up the back of the ball to counter the backspin and in the process you change the spin to topspin. Pushers usually stay quite close to the table (unlike a chopper who will go back and keep defending), so if you get a loop attack on the table you pose the pusher a problem. The pusher can't push again, as the ball has lots of topspin. You force the pusher to play a topspin game, where she may not be so comfortable. A weaker pusher may struggle to return your loop attacks and you will win points outright. A better pusher may be able to block your loop attacks, but at least you are changing the dynamics of the match - changing the rallies from backspin to topspin.

2. Return serves with flicks - Often, a pusher will serve short or half-long backspin serves. This makes sense for the pusher. She wants to start the rally as backspin, to make it easier to keep on pushing. So, an effective tactic is to return these serves by flicking. Once again you are changing the spin from backspin to topspin. It doesn't have to be an amazing super-fast flick which whizzes past the pusher. A basic flick will often do. You are simply changing the rhythm and speed of the rally. The pusher wants to play backspin. You change it to topspin. From my experience, even a basic backhand flick is enough to unsettle a pusher. The pusher will often struggle to adjust to the speed and spin of the service return, and will make a mistake, or play a weak shot giving you another opportunity to attack.

3. Use topspin serves - Pushers aren't usually strong attackers (this is why they push), so you should use plenty of topspin serves. Both short topspin serves and long topspin serves can be effective. If you serve topspin, it makes it much harder for a pusher to return the ball back short and low. If a pusher does attempt to push your topspin serve, it will most likely come back high, giving you an easy ball to attack. Some weaker pushers may struggle to return topspin serves at all. Stronger pushers, will be able to adjust to your topspin serves and may start blocking or driving the serves back. But at least you have changed the dynamics of the game again. You have changed it from a backspin game (the pusher's comfort zone) to a topspin game, which will hopefully favour you.

~

The chopper

A chopper is similar to a pusher. Both are defensive players and both like to play with backspin. The big difference is that a chopper will play further back from the table and use a more exaggerated swing (a chop) to return your attacks. Playing further back from the table gives a chopper more time to react to your attacks. When he chops, the ball can be returned with very heavy backspin, making it hard for you to attack again. Choppers are very consistent. They can keep a rally going for a long time, returning attack after attack. The chopper mainly wins points through your attacking mistakes. Some advanced level choppers will vary chops and topspin attacks. It can be quite unsettling when the defender switches to attack mode.

Tactics to beat a chopper

1. Play short, then long - A chopper likes to play back from the table. This gives the chopper space and time to play his chops, which requires an exaggerated swing. You can disrupt a chopper's rhythm and timing by moving him in and out of the table. Instead of trying to attack every chop, you can alternate between topspins and pushes. You attack.

The chopper returns with a chop. If you push the next ball short, the chopper will have to move close to the table. Now the chopper is out of position. If you now attack deep, the chopper will have to work harder to get back into position to chop again. You can keep repeating this trick - short, then long; short, then long. It is much harder for the chopper to play good defence if he has to keep moving in and out of the table.

2. Attack the wide zones - Since a chopper likes to play back from the table, he has to cover a wider area. This makes him vulnerable to wide balls. Try to place your attacks close to the side of the table. This will send the chopper very wide to chop the ball back. If the chopper cannot reach this very wide ball, you win the point. Even if the chopper can reach the ball, you have opened up a huge area on the table to aim your next shot. You are controlling the rally. Ideally, you should hit these wide shots with some speed. This makes it very difficult for the chopper to react, move and get a decent chop back on the table.

3. Use flatter attacks - A chopper usually finds it easier to return a topspin attack. He has a bit more time to react as the ball loops up and down. He can use all this topspin to his advantage, turning it into a heavy backspin chop. When the opportunity arises, usually when the ball is a little higher or has a little less backspin, try attacking with a flatter contact. Hit through the ball a bit more. You will be able to play a faster attack with more power. This is harder for the chopper to return. The ball moves towards the chopper quicker, and he has less spin to work with. When you flatten out the attack and add this extra power, the chopper will often struggle to return the ball. But you need patience. You have to pick the right ball. If the ball is low and loaded with heavy backspin, it is safer to loop the ball up. If the next ball comes back higher, then you can be more direct with your attack.

~

The blocker

A blocker is another defensive player. Unlike pushers and choppers, a blocker likes to play topspin rallies. But instead of attacking, a blocker will stay close to the table and block, block, block all day long. Playing a skilled blocker is like playing a brick wall. Everything comes back. A blocker seems to know where you're going to attack even before you've played your shot. You put all the effort in, topspinning this way and that way, but the ball keeps being returned. By the end of the match you're exhausted and dripping in sweat. You look across the table and the blocker is fresh as a daisy. What the heck? A blocker is not easy to beat. She uses your speed and spin against you. She can rush you. She can slow you down. She can move you all over the table. She disrupts your attacking flow and makes it difficult to play continuous attacks. Not easy at all.

Tactics to beat a blocker

1. Attack down the line - A blocker finds it easier if you always attack the same position. Many players have a habit of always attacking cross-court with their forehand. This is heaven for a blocker. A blocker can anticipate the attack, move into position early and simply block the ball back fast, slow, left, right or anywhere she wants. Try to attack cross-court *and* down the line. This makes it much harder for the blocker to anticipate where you are going to attack. Attacks down the line can be very effective. This is the shorter part of the table. The blocker has less time to react. If you attack with pace down the line, you can win many points, even against a very good blocker.

2. Attack the crossover position with speed - A blocker is usually vulnerable to fast attacks aimed at the crossover position, i.e. her playing elbow / hip. This is because the blocker has to decide whether to block with her forehand or backhand. The speed of the attack is important. If the attack is too slow, the blocker will have more time to move one way or another to block the ball back. If you attack the crossover position with speed, the blocker has far less time to react. You will jam the blocker up in the middle and force her to make an awkward block or make an error. Your point.

3. Vary the tempo - A blocker finds it easy if you always attack with medium speed and medium spin. She knows what to expect. The blocker can fix her bat angle and then block, block, block, block. No problem. However, if you vary the speed and spin of your attacks, she will find it much harder. Try some slow spinny loops. Try some flatter attacks with a bit more power. You will force the blocker to continually change her bat angle, timing and stroke length of the block. Some blockers struggle with slow topspin. Most blockers hate powerful flat hits. Experiment and see what works. In general, if you vary the rhythm and the tempo of your attacks, the blocker will make more errors.

The lobber

A lobber likes to play back from the table and will keep lobbing the ball up high over the net, inviting you to smash the ball. Doesn't sound too difficult, right? Well, a good lobber can be infuriating to play against. He will vary the height, depth and spin of his lobs. Some lobs will have a good kick of topspin. Some lobs will have a heavy dose of sidespin. Even when you smash the ball back, the lobber will chase the ball down and throw in another high lob. The lobber wins points through your smashing errors. Or if you play a weak shot, the lobber may counter-attack with a fast topspin. Lobbers are rarer. You don't find that many players who choose lobbing as their default playing style, but they do exist. And there are plenty of others who use lobbing as a back-up option if their preferred playing style isn't working.

Tactics to beat a lobber

1. Hit the ball hard - Power is by far the most effective way to beat a lobber. The ball is up in the air. You have a big margin to get the ball over the net. This is your opportunity to smash the ball hard. Don't bother adding topspin to your smashes. This will slow down the smash and the lobber will have more time to react. Smash the ball with a flat contact and hard. The ball will move faster and bounce higher and the lobber will have to work much harder at returning the ball. The size of the court is often quite small in amateur table tennis. If you smash the ball hard and flat, you will send the lobber to the back of the court, and he may run out of space to play his lobs. Try smashing into the corners to really maximise the area the lobber has to cover to return the ball.

2. Use drop shots - If you can't power through a lobber, try mixing in some drop shots. This is where you softly contact the ball straight after the bounce. It's a tricky shot, but if you execute it well, the ball will land short on the lobber's side. The lobber will have to rush into the table to keep the rally going. If the lobber is too far back, he might not reach the ball (or even attempt to reach the ball). Your point. If the lobber does reach the ball, he is now close to the table and probably slightly off-balance. Play your next shot deep or wide and you can control the rally.

3. Play a backspin game - If the first two options don't work, try turning the match into a backspin game. The lobber prefers topspin rallies, which allows him to play back from the table. Play a short backspin game instead. Serve short backspin. Return serves with short backspin. Keep your pushes tight. This will keep the lobber close to the table. Then when the opportunity arises, go for your attack. The lobber will have to defend from closer to the table and will find it much harder to use his annoying high lobs. Even if the lobber does manage some high lobs, you could try doing a backspin smash. This is where you chop down the side of the ball. This makes the ball swerve and float with a mixture of sidespin and backspin. The change of spin and speed can unsettle the lobber. He may not know how to return this type of smash. Your point.

The topspin attacker

A topspin attacker is a very common playing style, especially at the higher levels of amateur table tennis. As the name applies, a topspin attacker likes to play topspin strokes. Lots of them. If you push a ball, she topspins. If you block a ball, she topspins. Even if you topspin a ball, she topspins back. She is usually very confident with both forehand and backhand topspin, although one wing may be stronger than the other. Her goal is to impose her topspin game on you. She wants to turn every point into a topspin rally where she can play her favourite shots. She is not a fan of pushing. She prefers to flick or loop - changing the rally from backspin to topspin - as soon as possible. When you play a topspin attacker, you often feel like you are on the back foot. She always seems to attack first and the topspins are relentless. Most topspin attackers like the rallies to be fast, although you do get some slower, more controlled topspin attackers too.

Tactics to beat a topspin attacker

1. Use heavy backspin - The topspin attacker is usually comfortable attacking light and medium backspin balls, but will often struggle with very heavy backspin. Try serving short with lots of backspin to the forehand. Or push deep and aggressively with lots of backspin to the backhand. Or push wide with lots of backspin to the forehand. These are the three areas where you will have most success. The topspin attacker will still try to attack, but if she is weak in these areas, she will make errors and continue to do so, as this is the only way she plays. If she loses confidence she may start pushing instead, giving you the opportunity to attack first. Even if the topspin attacker can handle heavy backspin, she will most likely play slower topspin shots, which are easier to deal with.

2. Block or counter-hit with speed - If the backspin tactic doesn't work, and you can't stop a topspin attacker from topspinning, don't panic. Let her attack, but return her topspins with fast blocks or counter-hits. The speed is important. If your blocks are too slow, the topspin attacker will dominate the rallies. But if you inject some speed, you will really test her recovery and rallying skills. You need to be brave and stay close to the table, so you can block or counter-hit the ball early and play fast. She will have less time to prepare for her topspin strokes. When she feels your speed pressure, her shots may become jerky and rushed, resulting in more errors. Aim for the corners, the crossover position and keep switching the direction of play. This will stretch the topspin attacker and make her feel very uncomfortable.

3. Attack first - Don't be too intimidated by a topspin attacker. If the opportunity arises, try to attack first. This can completely change the dynamic of the game. When a topspin attacker worries about your attacks, her own topspin game can start to falter. She may stiffen up, rush her attacks or go for risky shots which are beyond her ability level (and miss!). A topspin attacker spends so much time topspinning, she doesn't always have a strong defensive game. If you attack first, you may find it quite easy to win points, as the topspin attacker struggles to return your attacks.

~

The mid-distance looper

The mid-distance looper is similar to a topspin attacker, but he likes to play further back from the table. He uses exaggerated topspin strokes. Big body rotation, big backswing and big follow-through too. He can generate a tremendous amount of topspin. The ball loops up over the net and kicks up violently off the table. His shots look very stylish, almost like a professional player. If a mid-distance looper connects cleanly, and places the ball well, he may well loop the ball past you for a clean winner. Everyone in the room will applaud this spectacular shot. Whilst a mid-distance looper looks amazing, he does have a few weaknesses you can exploit. The three tactics I suggested for the topspin attacker, may work against a mid-distance looper too, but here are three more which I like to use.

Tactics to beat a mid-distance looper

1. Keep the ball short and low - A mid-distance looper will back away from the table. This gives him the space he needs to execute his big looping strokes. You can frustrate a mid-distance looper by playing a short game. Serve short, return short and push short. If you keep the ball short and low, you will force the mid-distance looper to play close to the table, and he will find it much harder to use his loops. This is frustrating for the mid-distance looper. If he doesn't have a strong game close to the table, he will make attacking errors or play weak shots, giving you the opportunity to attack. When you have the mid-distance looper jammed up close to the table, you can play an occasional deep push or flick. This sudden change of length can often catch him out.

2. Use slow blocks - When a mid-distance looper is looping away from the table, try taking the pace off the ball with slow blocks. This is my favourite tactic. The mid-distance looper wants the ball to come through with a bit of speed, but when you play a slow block, the ball drops much shorter. It dips as it reaches him. He now has to adjust his timing and swing and his big loops suddenly become erratic. As he stumbles forwards to reach this slower ball, he may completely mess up his loop. Your point. Mixing up slow blocks and fast blocks can be very effective at keeping the mid-distance looper off balance.

3. Attack the wide zones - As he likes to go back from the table, the mid-distance looper has to cover a larger area. If you play your shots very wide, he will have to move quite a distance to get to the ball. If his footwork is not very good, the mid-distance looper may not be able to reach the ball. Your point. However, most mid-distance loopers do have pretty decent footwork. There's not much point playing at mid-distance if you can't move well. So assume he will get to your wide balls. But now he will be far outside the table, giving you a great opportunity to target your next shot at the big open space on the other side of the table. Make the mid-distance looper scamper left and right. Wear him out. He may hit the odd screaming loop past you, but in general he will find it much harder to play his powerful loops when moving to these wide positions.

~

The one-wing attacker

A one-wing attacker almost always attacks only with his stronger side. Most commonly, the strong side is the forehand. He uses his good footwork and service tactics to set up his strong side again and again. If you play the ball to his weaker backhand, he steps around and whizzes a forehand past you. If you try to catch him out with a ball to his wide forehand, he quickly steps across and whizzes another ball past you. No matter where you put the ball, the one-wing attacker always seems to be able to attack with his strong side.

Tactics to beat a one-wing attacker

1. Target the weak side relentlessly - Let's assume the one-wing attacker has a strong forehand and a weaker backhand. If this is the case, you should target his weaker backhand again and again. Serve to his backhand. Return serves to his backhand. Keep rallying to his backhand. Give him as few chances as possible to play with his stronger forehand. A good one-wing forehand attacker will be able to cover most of the table with his forehand. So, try to play very wide to his backhand. This will make it harder for him to step around. Don't feel apologetic about targeting his backhand. It may be your best chance of winning. If it works, just keep doing it. The one-wing attacker leaves you very little choice. If you play to his forehand you will likely get beat. You have to exploit the weaker backhand over and over again.

2. Play quick shots to the open table - A one-wing attacker will often try to play forehands from the backhand corner. This allows him to use his stronger side, but it does create a lot of space on the table. He is now vulnerable to quick blocks or counter attacks to the opposite corner. Try to target this open space. If you contact the ball early, the one-wing attacker will have to move very quickly to reach the ball. If he doesn't move quick enough, you can hit clean winners. He may then become more reluctant to play his forehand from the backhand corner. You have caused doubt in his mind. He may even start using his weaker backhand instead. Now you are controlling the match.

3. Mess with his mind! - If you force the one-wing attacker to frequently use his weaker backhand side, his stronger forehand may become less reliable too. As you have given him few opportunities to use his forehand, when you do play to his stronger side, he may feel added pressure to perform. This can make him tense up and rush the shot. He hasn't had many chances to use his forehand, so he may try too hard - overcompensate too much - and make an error. You have truly messed with his mind. You have forced him to use his weaker backhand most of the time and when he does use his forehand, it has fallen to pieces. You win.

The flat hitter

A flat hitter will attack the ball with a very flat contact, rather than topspin. You play a slightly loose shot and then BHAM! The ball gets smashed past you. You trudge off to the back of the court to collect the ball. Next point, BHAM! The ball flies past you again. It can be demoralising getting smashed off the table by a flat hitter. Her attacks are fast, powerful and difficult to return. It's not easy to react to the speed of her flat hits. Even if you do get to the ball, the lack of spin makes it difficult to block the ball back. A flat hitter can be inconsistent. In one game she will miss many attacks. In the next game all the attacks go in. If you play a flat hitter when she is on form, you can be in big trouble.

Tactics to beat a flat hitter

1. Keep the ball low - It is more difficult for a flat hitter to attack balls which are low. This is because she hits the ball in a straight line, rather than spinning the ball up over the net. If the ball is low, there is less margin to flat hit a ball over the net and get it to touch the other side of the table. A low, deep push, loaded with backspin, will be nearly impossible to flat hit. But a floaty push, which is a little high, is easy for a flat hitter to attack. A fast, low topspin is harder for a flat hitter to attack. A slow topspin which goes higher over the net is easier for a flat hitter to attack. A return of serve which is kept low = harder. A return of serve which pops up high = easy. You get the idea. A flat hitter can only attack effectively if the ball is high enough. So keep the ball low.

2. Play quick shots - A flat hitter loves it when the play is a little slow, e.g. floaty pushes, steady blocks or slow topspin attacks. To generate power, a flat hitter often uses a longer stroke and will put plenty of her body into the shot. This is much easier to do if the ball is slow, as she has time to get her feet, body and bat into position to hit the ball hard. Try to play with speed and rush her with fast pushes, blocks and topspins. It is a lot harder for the flat hitter to set herself up for the big hit, when she has less time. You will force her to use shorter, jerkier strokes. If your placement is good, she will have to hit whilst off-balance too. When you inject speed into the rallies, the flat hitter will make more attacking errors, or may choose not to attack, allowing you to dominate the rallies.

3. Be assertive - When you play a very aggressive flat hitter, there is a temptation to play passively. You become more concerned with her aggression, rather than focusing on your game. You may find that your strokes become a bit tentative. The result? You will play weaker shots and then BHAM!, the ball is smashed past you again. So, you must put the flat hitter under pressure and give her something to worry about too. If you're usually an attacker, keep playing your attacking game. Play fast topspins to different positions on the table. If you're usually a defender, keep the ball low with heavy backspin and you will force errors. Keep the pressure on. A flat hitter can be very inconsistent, but only if you make the game hard for her.

The long pimples player

One of the trickiest opponents you will face in amateur table tennis is the player who uses long pimples. The long pimples alter the spin on the ball in a way which is different to a regular inverted rubber. I clearly remember my first match against a long pimples player. I simply didn't have a clue what was going on. My pushes were popping up really high. My blocks were hitting the bottom of the net. My attacks were going long or into the net – anywhere other than my opponent's half of the table. It was like I'd forgotten how to play table tennis. This is the goal of the long pimples player. The rubber causes confusion. It messes with your mind. When you start doubting yourself, you hesitate. When you hesitate, you play weak shots. When you play weak shots, you lose points.

Before I share my top three tactics to beat a long pimples player, it's important to understand how the spin changes. As a general guide:

- If you play a heavy topspin attack and the long pimples player chops, you get a heavy backspin return
- If you play a light topspin attack and the long pimples player chops, you get a medium/light backspin return
- If you play a topspin attack and the long pimples player blocks, you get a float return
- If you do a medium backspin push and the long pimples player pushes, you get a float return

- If you do a heavy backspin push and the long pimples player pushes, you get a float/light topspin return

It's all back to front and confusing. It's often the opposite to what you expect, but it is predictable. When you have an understanding of what effect the long pimples are having on the ball, you need to work out what you're going to do about it. This means you need to change your style of play. There's no point playing the same way against a long pimples player as you would against a player with inverted rubbers. The ball is reacting to the long pimples differently, so you *have* to play differently.

Tactics to beat a long pimples player

1. Topspin, push, topspin, push - If you play a topspin attack and the long pimples player chops, the ball comes back with very heavy backspin. It's physically very demanding to keep playing consecutive topspin attacks, as each time the ball is returned with ever more backspin. More often than not, you'll run out of steam and topspin the ball into the net. One tactic to overcome this is to alternate topspin and push shots. You attack with topspin, your opponent chops with long pimples. Instead of topspinning the heavy backspin ball, just push the ball back. Your opponent will most likely push and the ball will come back to you with no spin or light topspin. This is much easier to attack than heavy backspin. You can play more direct attacks, with more power and try to finish the point. You may need to play this combination a few times – topspin, push, topspin, push - until there is an easy ball to hit for a winner.

2. Attack high floaty balls with flat hits – You will often get floaty balls – balls with little spin – which are a little high. This is your chance to break from the topspin, push routine and win the point. When you get a floaty ball which is a little high, don't attack with topspin. Instead, hit the ball with a flatter contact. You will be able to hit the ball harder and faster, giving the long pimples player less time and space to chop back. Aim for the corners or the crossover position, and he will find it difficult to play his chop shots with any consistency or high quality.

3. Play with light spin - If the first two tactics don't work for you, you could try playing a slower game with very little spin. Play with light topspin attacks and light backspin pushes. By using light spin, you won't get heavy spin returns, and it's much easier to keep the rally going for longer. This style of play does require a lot of patience. The rallies can be quite long, as you wait for an easy ball to attack with speed. But I've often found that a long pimples player will get frustrated against this style of play, as he doesn't have much spin to work with. He may start forcing his strokes too much and make unforced errors. What a refreshing change!

The short pimples player

Short pimples are a little easier to understand than long pimples. The spin doesn't change to the same degree. When a short pimples player attacks or blocks or pushes, the ball won't have much spin. It will be the expected spin, just less of it. If a short pimples player loops, the ball will have light topspin. If she blocks, the ball will be floaty. If she pushes it will have light backspin. The short pimples player likes to play close to the table and is usually quite aggressive. She can't generate much spin, but she can hit through your topspin shots. She can hit through short spinny serves. She can hit through floaty pushes. The short pimples player likes to hit hard and fast. This gives you little time to react. As this spin is different to an inverted rubber, it is easy to panic and make an error.

Tactics to beat a short pimples player

1. Keep the ball deep - A short pimples player wants to play close to the table. This makes it easier to hit balls at the top of the bounce, where she has the biggest margin to get her hits over the net. If she goes back too far from the table, then it becomes harder to hit the ball at the top of the bounce. Her hits become more risky. So try to play your balls deep - really close to the end of the table. This gives the short pimples player little time to react. Use a few more long serves. Keep them low and fast. Don't worry too much about spin. Just get the serves deep.

When you push - push deep. When you attack - attack deep. If you can keep the ball low, then even better. This will make it very hard for the short pimples player to hit at the top of the bounce. If she tries, she will make more errors. Or if she backs away from the table, she won't be able to use her short pimples effectively.

2. Use heavy backspin pushes - A short pimples player doesn't usually loop that well. This is why she uses short pimples. Even if she can loop, the loop will have less spin compared to an inverted rubber. If you use heavy backspin pushes - especially deep pushes - you may be able to stop the short pimples player from attacking. She can't flat hit, as the ball is too low. She will either push back, giving you the opportunity to attack or she will attempt a loop, which won't have much spin, giving you the opportunity to counter-attack. Don't think you are being negative by using more pushes than usual. It's just a simple tactic to stop a short pimples player from attacking, and also a way of setting up your own attacks.

3. Play topspin-drives - A short pimples player likes a bit of topspin to hit through, especially when the topspin sits up a little high. She then has a bigger margin to hit through the ball. So, when you attack, try being more direct. Use topspin-drives. A bit of spin and a bit of hit. These attacks will be faster, less spinny and lower. The speed causes problems, as the short pimples player is close to the table and will have less time to react. The flatter contact and lowness makes it hard for her to counter-hit. You will force the short pimples player to defend. If you attack with good placement - corners or the crossover - you will win many points.

Even if she does block the ball back, the ball will be floaty, giving you the chance to topspin-drive again.

~

The anti-spin player

Our final player is rare and quite deceptive. Anti-spin rubber looks like a normal inverted rubber, but it plays very differently. Basically, it kills any spin you put on the ball. Your best spinny serve has no effect. Your heavy forehand loop has no effect. Your aggressive backhand push has no effect. No matter how much you spin, the ball is returned to you with very little spin at all. Usually, the anti-spin player will use an anti-spin rubber on the backhand and an inverted rubber on the forehand. The backhand is used to defend and confuse. The forehand is used to attack any weak shots. Sometimes you come across a player who uses anti-spin rubbers on both sides - like Roger who I described in the previous chapter. These players won't attack much, but will just keep returning balls until you get frustrated and make a mistake. They can be infuriating to play against.

Tactics to beat an anti-spin player

1. Hit the ball hard - The best tactic is power. There's not much point trying to beat an anti-spin player with lots of spinny shots. He can return these with ease. You need to use some power. This is fairly easy to do, as you will get lots of floaty balls to attack. The anti-spin player can't generate much spin. Every ball he gives you with his anti-spin rubber will have no-spin or very little spin. Serve fast and deep to the anti-spin rubber. The ball will come back with no-spin. Then be aggressive with the third ball. Either drive the ball or add a little topspin, but make sure the shot is more hit than spin. The extra pace and power will make it hard for the anti-spin player to return your attack. Don't get tempted to lift the ball too much, even if the anti-spin player pushes. Remember, the ball won't have much spin, so your loop will likely go off the end of the table. You need to attack more forwards than up. Be direct and aggressive.

2. Play close to the table - An anti-spin push, chop or block usually slows the ball down. The ball doesn't come through at the pace you expect. This catches many players out. Try staying a little closer to the table and really watch the flight of the ball. You will need to adjust your timing. Don't rush. Don't panic. Wait for the ball to reach the peak of the bounce and then power through the shot. This is much easier to do if you are standing closer to the table. If you are too far back, you will have to contact the ball as it is dropping, which means you have to spin the ball more. This is what the anti-spin player wants. Stay close and be aggressive.

3. Stay focused - Anti-spin can be effective because it messes with your muscle memory. You see a player push the ball and your mind processes what it sees and tells your body what to do (either push or loop). But with anti-spin you have to override your muscle memory. If you push a no-spin ball in the same way you push a backspin ball, it will pop up high. If you loop a no-spin ball in the same way as you loop a backspin ball, it will go off the end of the table. You need to stay alert. Keep telling yourself that the ball has no-spin. And adjust your stroke accordingly. It's OK if you make a mistake. Stay calm. Remind yourself the ball has no-spin and try again.

Your tactical toolkit

The tactics I have shared in this chapter work for me. I have a playing style which combines pushes, blocks and topspin-drive attacks, playing close to the table. These are shots I can play well. Many of my tactics focus on using these shots. This is important. There is little point in me using tactics which require shots I cannot consistently do. For my tactics, there is no mention of forehand flicks, counter-topspins, chops or lobs. If I use these too much, I would play to my weaknesses.

You also need to play to your strengths, but every player has a different combination of strengths. Here is your homework. Take a few of the playing styles I have mentioned in this chapter - or all of them if you have time - and write down your top three tactics. If it helps, imagine a player you know who roughly fits the description of a playing style. Think through the tactics which usually work against this player and other new tactics you could try. Choose tactics which play to your strengths. Think through the ways you usually win points (as we discussed in Chapter 7). How can your strengths and point winning methods be applied to each different playing style?

You may come up with similar tactics to me. Or you may come up with a completely different set of tactics for each playing style. It really doesn't matter. There is no right or wrong. Multiple different tactics could work with each playing style. By working through this analytical process - really thinking deeply about an opponent's potential weaknesses - you develop a much stronger tactical mindset. You won't always get it right. A fair amount of trial and error is required. But if you are thinking about tactics, you will find it much easier to switch tactics when something isn't working. The goal is to find one or two tactics which enable you to compete with, and potentially beat, every opponent you play.

Put down this book. Pick up a pen and paper, switch on your tablet or open your laptop, and start writing your own tactical toolkit - based upon your own strengths. This toolkit is something you can keep referring back to - and updating - when you play your league matches and tournaments.

Playing matches

It's match time. You've worked hard in the training hall. Your serves are spinny and dangerous. You have some awesome point winning strategies. You have a clear and focused mind. Now all you have to do is put everything together and victory is yours. Simple.

Well, maybe not. Matches are a bit like walking in a very busy street. You know how to walk. You know where you want to go. But there are all these obstacles in your way making it harder for you to get to your destination. Many of these obstacles (the people) seem to move in unpredictable ways. Some slow. Some fast. Some suddenly change direction. What seems like a simple task is actually a bit stressful. Everything is a bit chaotic. A bit random.

This is your typical table tennis match. A bit chaotic and a bit random. You know how to play pushes, drives and topspins, but the player on the other side of the table - your opponent - is an obstacle. He doesn't give you nice balls where you can show off your wonderful technique. He puts the ball into unexpected positions. He gives you nasty spin. He changes the pace. He is unpredictable. He makes it hard for you to reach your table tennis destination - match point and victory.

How do we make sense of all this? How can we try to tame the randomness? How can we play well in matches, replicating what we do in a more relaxed training environment? In this chapter, I try to answer these questions. I am going to share a mixture of physical, tactical and psychological tips to help you play as well as you can, when it matters most - in a competitive match. We're going to look at how to do a good warm-up, how to analyse an opponent, how to implement a game plan, how to handle pressure and how to win matches. Are you ready? Let's play!

Warm-up

If you play league table tennis, you've probably encountered this scenario. You've had a hard day at work. You rush home. You grab something to eat. You rush out again. You travel to your match (car, bike, tube or bus). Sometimes the traffic is heavy, sometimes not. By the time you get to the venue, you only have five minutes to warm up. You hit a few balls forehand to forehand, and then some backhand to backhand, but you're not focused. You're still a bit wound-up by your hectic day. Then the matches begin. Your first match isn't great. You're a bit tight and tense and you don't play anywhere near your best level. You moan to yourself, or your teammates, about your lack of a proper warm-up.

Tournaments can also be a challenge. There is usually more scope for a longer warm-up, but not always. With lots of players competing for table space to warm up, you might not get that much time. You often have to share the table - four players warming up simultaneously. This severely restricts the quality of the warm-up.

In an ideal world, you would have at least 30 minutes to warm up properly with just two players per table. But in 13 years of table tennis, I have very rarely had the opportunity to warm up for 30 minutes. Far more common is only having five minutes. This is clearly not ideal, but it's the reality most of us face. One solution is to get to a venue earlier for a longer warm-up, but this isn't always possible. You have to accept that sometimes – many times – you're only going to have five minutes to warm up on the table. Rather than feeling overly negative about this, you should switch your focus to how you can make the most of these five minutes to get ready for a match.

The five-minute warm-up

This is how to warm up for a competitive match if you only have five minutes. Start with a cross-court knock-up. Forehand to forehand and backhand to backhand. This will help you get a feel for the table, the ball and the general conditions. Start with a few drives at a medium pace and then build up to a faster rally, using some topspin if you like. Try to loosen the body and increase your heart rate. After you've hit a few balls, start varying where you place the ball, so you and your partner have to move to play shots. This will get your feet working and get you energised.

It's very tempting to spend five minutes just hitting cross-court, but don't waste all your time doing this. There are better ways to prepare for a match, even if you only have a few minutes. When you have spent a short time playing cross-court, move on to warming up your biggest strength. You want to get this shot in good shape for the start of the

don't waste it. Warm up more of the shots you like to play - loops, pushes, blocks, flicks, serves and return of serves. If I have more time, I always try to warm up my backhand loop, which is a weak shot. I usually miss my first attempt, but after three or four efforts, the shot starts to work and is ready for the start of the match. With additional warm-up time, I will often play a practice game or two. The score doesn't matter, I just want to prepare myself for the randomness of match-play.

Have a think about your warm-ups. What would your ideal warm-up be, if you only had five minutes? What shots do you want to get working before a match starts? You don't need to over-complicate this. As always, keep it simple. Just focus on a few things which will get your heart rate up, get you moving your feet and increase your confidence. Also have a think about how you would warm up if you have 10 minutes, 20 minutes or 30 minutes. What extra activities would you do? Whether you have five minutes or 30 minutes, try to warm up with a purpose and you will get off to a flying start when the match begins.

Analysing your opponent

In an ideal world, you would know everything about your opponent. Her playing style, her strengths, her weaknesses, how she serves, how she returns serves, whether she prefers backspin or topspin rallies. Sometimes you do know all of this because you have played an opponent many times before. You only need to do the briefest of analysis to remind yourself of who you are playing and what tactics you should use.

The tougher challenge comes when your opponent is someone you have never played before. Before I start a match, I want some idea of what I'm dealing with. At a minimum I want to know the playing style of my opponent. If I know the playing style, I have some ready-made tactics which I can try (see Chapter 8). For example, I turn up for a league match. I have a warm-up - only five minutes as we are already running late! My first opponent I have never played before. I have heard about her, though. She is a chopper, with a fierce reputation. Bingo! I know a few tactics to play against a chopper. I can start the match with a game plan.

To work out an opponent's playing style is fairly easy. You just need to observe. If you are playing a league match - and it's your turn to sit out - then put down your mobile phone. That WhatsApp message can wait. Instead, pay attention to the opponent you are due to play. Does she broadly fit with one of the categories described in the previous chapter? If so, great. You already have some tactics which may work. It's the same principle if you are playing in a tournament. There is usually lots of spare time during a tournament. Spend some of this time watching potential opponents. Once again, match up each opponent with a category from Chapter 8 and think through the tactics which may work.

Deeper analysis

If you take the time and effort to observe an opponent playing, you can do more than just identify the playing style. You can do a deeper analysis. This is what I look for:

1. The weaker side - is my opponent stronger on the forehand side or the backhand side? If there is a big discrepancy, e.g. the backhand is much weaker, I will target that side much more.

2. Footwork - How well does my opponent move? Does she reach for wide balls or does she move her feet? If the footwork is obviously poor, I know that wide balls, short balls and balls to the crossover position are likely to be highly effective.

3. Looping skills - Can my opponent attack backspin balls well? If not, I know that some heavy backspin serves and some heavy backspin pushes will make it hard for her to attack.

4. Defensive skills - Can my opponent defend well? Does she try to block or take wild attacking swings? If I suspect her defensive skills are lacking, I know I should attack a little more. I may win some easy points.

From this deeper analysis, I can refine my game plan further. Let's say I am due to play a topspin attacker. I quickly identified the playing style by watching her play. I know how to play against a topspin attacker from previous experience. I have some general tactics which usually work, but for this opponent I have observed some extra weaknesses. Her backhand is weaker than her forehand. So, I'm going to keep much of the play to her backhand side. I noticed she can hit a topspin ball quite well, but struggles to loop backspin. So, I'm going to serve a bit more backspin to her backhand and push her serves also to her backhand. This will make it hard for her to attack. Her defence is erratic. She jumps back from the table and either tries to swing at the ball or sometimes starts lobbing. So, when I attack, I should try to get the ball wide, and she will struggle to reach the ball. I now have a game plan to start the match. I have taken my established tactics from Chapter 8, and refined them with the new insight I have gained from observing my opponent play. I am ready to go.

When you observe your opponent, you may be looking for weaknesses, which are different to what I look for. This is absolutely fine. It all depends on your playing style and your point winning strategies. But try to keep it simple. Don't overload your brain with too much information. Try to identify one or two potential weaknesses which you can exploit.

Unknown opponent

A tougher challenge is playing an opponent who you know nothing about. You have never played before. You've had no opportunity to

Game plan

You've warmed-up. You have analysed your opponent. You know his playing style. You have identified a couple of potential weaknesses. You have two or three tactics in mind. Not every point is going to play out as you expect. It's random match-play after all, but your tactical focus will tame some of the randomness. This is your game plan. Your Plan A.

Plan A

Let's flesh this out with a hypothetical example. I am playing a flat hitting attacker. He hits very hard and consistently with his forehand, but his backhand seems a bit erratic. I have observed he will push a backspin ball, rather than loop. Plus he doesn't seem to move very well for wide balls. For my tactics, I am going to take a simple approach:

1. Use lots of backspin - Serve backspin and use heavy backspin pushes. This will make it hard for him to attack.

2. Play to his backhand - His forehand is strong. I need to keep it away from that side. I will tie him up on his backhand side.

Just two tactics and a clear focus - backspin and backhand. This will make it hard for him to attack and hopefully frustrate him as he can't use his strongest shot. He will make some errors. Should I attack? Yes, if the opportunity arises, but I am prepared to push a couple of extra balls and choose the right ball to loop. Let's just see how it goes, but initially I want to keep my focus on using backspin and targeting his backhand.

The match begins. Success! The tactics are working. His backhand is erratic - more than expected. He is making lots of errors and is starting to shout at himself. His pushing is weak as well. He can get his pushes over the net - most of the time - but his pushes are floaty, which are easy for me to attack. He seems desperate to get his big forehand flat hit into the match, but I won't let him. I win the first game 11-6. The next game follows a similar pattern. I tie him up on the backhand side. He is unable to use his forehand. He tries attacking my heavy pushes, but his shots are wild. One or two land on the table, but he misses far more. I win the next game 11-6 again. I don't feel there is a need to change my tactical approach. For the next game I focus mostly on backhand and backspin again. He is really losing the plot now. Wild swings, poor body language and lots of grumbles. He seems to be giving up. I decide to attack a little more, just to add to his misery. I win comfortably. The final score is 11-6, 11-6, 11-4. The game planned worked beautifully.

Plan B

This is what can happen when everything goes right. You congratulate yourself on devising and implementing such a successful game plan. You are a tactical genius! However, not all table tennis matches go exactly to plan. Your opponent is not a one-dimensional robot. He will also be experimenting with tactics. He will be capable of changing playing style if necessary. He will be trying to find a way to win. What happens if your Plan A doesn't work?

Let's restart the hypothetical example. This time the flat hitting attacker is stronger than I expected. I thought his backhand was erratic, but he seems to have found some consistency and his confidence is growing. My tactic of targeting the backhand isn't helping me much. He is also adjusting to my backspin tactic and is starting to loop. His loops are slow and spinny, and I am having trouble keeping my blocks low. He then flat hits the ball fast and hard and I can't return. I try putting the balls wider, as I had observed his footwork wasn't strong. Maybe that will change things? No, he seems to be moving fine now. I am becoming too predictable, and he has found his attacking rhythm. I lose the first game 11-7, and I am losing 6-3 in the second game.

What should I do? I could continue with Plan A, hoping the flat hitter will start missing. Maybe I just need to execute Plan A better - use heavier backspin and mix up the ball placement more. However, the signs are not good. I am one game down and losing the second game. The flat hitter is playing with increasing confidence. I need to try something different. I need to switch to Plan B.

Switching strategies mid-game is not always easy to do, but has the potential to transform a match. In my mind, I always have a Plan B to fall back on if things aren't going well. I seem to have a pretty good record of coming back from 2-0, to win a match 3-2. Maybe this means I keep getting my Plan A wrong - this is why I am losing 2-0. But at least I can turn a match around by switching strategies. My Plan B usually means being more aggressive by flicking or looping instead of pushing. I use more topspin serves and attempt stronger third ball attacks. I try to attack first and generally increase the tempo of my play.

Back to the hypothetical example. I am losing. I'm playing too passively. The flat hitter is starting to batter me. I have a stern but motivational word to myself. Time to change the tempo. Time to switch to Plan B - ATTACK! I serve fast with topspin. He wasn't expecting this. The ball is returned passively. I hit the ball fast, with spin into the corner. Interesting. He didn't move for that ball. Maybe his footwork is not strong when the pace is faster. He serves short. I flick to his crossover position. He is surprised again by the change of pace and makes an error. I loop instead of push. His defence is weak. I win a few points. I am back in the second game. The score is now 9-9, and it's my serve. A thought creeps into my mind. Maybe I should play it safe again. I'm back in the game. I don't want to throw this away. Maybe he will make a mistake now. No, Tom, no! You must keep up the tempo. My mind refocuses on Plan B. I do a topspin serve and strong third ball attack. My point. I then do the same serve, but to a different position. The flat hitter takes a wild swing and hits the ball into the net. My point and my game. It's now 1-1.

I have tried both Plan A and Plan B. It's clear which game plan is working. In the next game I continue with Plan B, playing lots of attacking table tennis. I win 11-4. This is getting comfortable now. In the next game, I mix things up, switching between Plan A and Plan B. This unpredictable play seems to be causing issues. When I push to his backhand, it is definitely more erratic now as he is trying too hard to win points. Next rally I play fast again. His confidence is draining. I see his head drop. I know I will win. Final score - 7-11, 11-9, 11-4, 11-5.

I would experience all the classic physical symptoms – heavy legs, breathlessness, tension in my shoulders, butterflies in the stomach and a dry mouth. The tension was the killer. It was like I couldn't move. I was just so tight. My shots would become jerky. A simple push would feel like a monumental struggle. A topspin shot would be pathetic. The tension in my muscles slowed down my arm movement, resulting in a short, tame stroke, which would often send the ball into the net. My legs would be stuck to the spot. I had no energy and it felt like a huge effort to move side to side. I would just reach out for the balls instead. My spinny serves would lose all spin as my tight grip would send the ball over with very little spin at all. And returning serves? Forget it! I would just tamely prod at the ball. The server's spin would dominate my rubber and I would have no control over where the ball went. My nervous state made me play terrible in many games. I would finish the match unable to explain to teammates why I played so badly, when they had seen me play so much better during practice matches.

I am certainly not alone. Many players find nerves quite debilitating. The extra anxiety in playing a competitive match can make their body and mind freeze, which can have a terrible impact on their performance. How can we cope with pressure? How can we control our nerves? I'm not a sports psychologist - just a humble table tennis coach. I don't have all the answers. There is a wealth of information - books, websites, videos - which suggest ideas to help you cope with pressure. I encourage you to do your own research. However, there is one tool, which has helped me immensely. This tool has helped me control my nerves and perform much better, much more often. This tool is mental rehearsal. It is a tool used by many professional athletes in all sports, but you don't need to be a professional athlete to experience the benefits of mental rehearsal. Any table tennis player, at any standard, can benefit.

What is mental rehearsal?

Mental rehearsal is where you play an imaginary movie in your mind of yourself playing table tennis to the best of your ability. This imaginary movie could be focused on one aspect of table tennis – executing a serve, doing a loop, playing a fast push, smashing a high ball or any stroke which you like. Or the movie could be a sequence – serve, recover, loop, recover, topspin down the line. In this movie, you are executing each stroke or movement to the best of your ability. You are playing your 'A' game.

Mental rehearsal helps to build and deepen the pathways in your brain, reinforcing the physical practice you do. These pathways provide the blueprint of how a shot should look, feel and sound. Your actual performance improves, as your physical actions strive to match the mental images you have created. Whilst this may sound a bit new-age and pseudoscience, there is actually tons of research about how effective mental rehearsal can be. Let's look at some practical examples of how you can use mental rehearsal when playing table tennis.

Day of the match - On the day of a league match or tournament, do not waste any time or energy worrying about the ability of your opponents and whether you will win or lose. This will increase your anxiety levels. Instead, play the movie in your mind of how you want to perform. Focus on two or three things you want to do really well when playing. Imagine in your mind how this looks, how it feels and how it sounds. Imagine in detail each aspect of a movement or stroke or sequence of strokes.

For me, I visualise myself staying low, on the front of my feet, playing spinny backhands and twisting when playing my forehands. I visualise myself making space on the table to play my forehand topspins (my strongest shot). Overall, I am visualising myself playing positive attacking table tennis, in a low stance with good footwork. This mental rehearsal helps get me into the right mindset. It prevents me from worrying about winning or losing. I still experience nerves, but a little more towards excitement nerves, rather than deep foreboding debilitating nerves.

Just before the match starts - A few minutes before a match starts is another opportunity for mental rehearsal. You will quite likely rehearse the same shots or movements as earlier in the day. It's the final reminder for your brain and body of how you want to perform. It's a great way of getting in the zone and keeping your nerves under control. It helps you to start a match quicker and to reach your best level early in a match.

Before serving - Mental rehearsal before serving is something I have found very beneficial. It's your serve. Take your time. Visualise the serve you are going to do and your recovery after the serve. Visualise how the serve is likely to be returned. Visualise your ideal third ball attack. Of course, you can't guarantee how your serve is going to be returned, but you should have an idea of the likely return. For example, I know a short backspin serve at my level, is very often returned with a push. So, I play the movie in my mind. I serve, recover, stay low, my opponent pushes the ball. I then execute a forehand loop and control the rally. This mental rehearsal makes it much easier to execute the serve and loop sequence. Since I have played the movie in my mind, I am in a better state of alertness. I am expecting the ball to be returned. I have already planned out my next move. Even if the ball is returned in a way I am not expecting, I can cope with it better because my mental state is sharper.

In between points - You have just lost a point with some poor play. It could be clumsy footwork, rushing your shots, hitting the ball too flat, a poorly executed loop or a weak block. Before the next point starts, you have an opportunity to refocus and rehearse the shot in your mind – reminding your body of what it should be doing. For example, when I get tight, my forehand topspin breaks down. I don't twist. Instead, I poke at the ball, playing a weak shot. If this happens, in between points, I imagine myself playing a forehand topspin properly – keeping low, rotating the core and accelerating forwards and up. This refocuses me and keeps my mindset positive. I am more likely to execute the forehand topspin properly the next time I attempt the shot.

Change of ends - At the end of a game, when you change ends, you have another opportunity for mental rehearsal. You may have identified a pattern during the previous game. For example, you missed five backhand loops – each one going into the net. Chances are you were too tight and rushed too much. But you know you can make this shot. Imagine how a backhand loop looks and feels. Play the movie in your mind of how you play a backhand loop when training. The mental rehearsal once again helps you refocus and re-establishes some self-belief.

Staying positive

Despite all the training, all the tactical preparation, all the mental rehearsal, things will still go wrong during some matches. This is the nature of competitive sport. You will make mistakes and find yourself in losing positions. But do not panic. If you maintain your focus on the process of playing - tactics and mental rehearsal - it is possible to overcome adversity and get back to playing your best.

Let's start with mistakes. We all make silly mistakes and unforced errors when playing table tennis, but there is often a big difference between how players respond to making a mistake. Some players dwell on the mistake and then make lots more mistakes. Other players seem unaffected by mistakes and bounce back stronger. How can we be more like the player who responds positively to mistakes?

I have a player I coach who can do a training drill brilliantly nine times in a row. But on the tenth attempt, he messes up. He will then say out loud "I can't do this drill". I can see the self-doubt in his facial expressions. His body becomes tense, and inevitably he will start making more mistakes. The same happens in a match. He will be playing well and winning. Then he makes a mistake and his self-doubting mind goes into overdrive. He will dwell on what he did wrong. His mind will flood with all the other times he has done it wrong. He will tell himself "I just can't play this shot. I always mess it up". His grip will tighten. His muscles tense up. His shots become rushed and jerky. And guess what?

He messes up even more. All the negative thinking becomes self-fulfilling. He tells himself he can't do it. He visualises other times he messed up, and he messes up again. His game unravels, and he loses the next few points.

This is actually quite common. Many players experience these feelings. We all make mistakes, but mistakes don't have to destroy your confidence. Instead, try using the mental rehearsal tool we discussed in the previous section:

- When you make a mistake in a match, pause for a moment.
- Quickly analyse why you made the error, but don't dwell on it.
- Instead, visualise how the shot should be played.
- Fill your mind with examples of when you have played the shot correctly.
- Physically re-enact how the shot should be played.
- Give yourself a brief positive instruction on what to do next time.

Here's a personal example. I have a bad habit of reaching forwards when attempting to play a backhand drive or backhand topspin. I am very aware of this. This habit often resurfaces in a match when the score is close. How do I deal with it? Firstly, I don't get stressed. It's no big deal. I pause and maybe walk away from the table. In a fairly detached way, I recognise I made the mistake by reaching forwards to the ball. I then start visualising how I want to play the shot – letting the ball come to me, keeping a loose wrist and elbow and spinning the ball. If I want more positive reinforcement, I think about the times in matches I have played this shot well. I may even shadow play the shot, to remind my body of what to do. I will give myself an instruction to "Wait for the ball, stay loose and spin". All of this just takes a few seconds – the time available between points.

The key here is to focus my mind on how to play the shot correctly, rather than dwelling on what I did wrong. By focusing my mind on how to play the shot, I increase the likelihood of actually doing the shot correctly the next time. I use this approach in training sessions, competitive matches – every time I play. I teach my mind to respond to mistakes in a positive and productive way.

Staying positive when losing

What about when you are losing? We all have bad games. There could be any number of reasons for a poor performance. Too nervous. Mind unfocused. Unfamiliar environment. Injured body part. Awkward playing style. Opponent too good. Whatever the reason, you're not playing well and you're losing. This often leads to frustration and poor decision-making. You make more errors. You get more disheartened. You start playing wild shots in a desperate attempt to get back in the match. The wild shots go into the net. More despondence. Your head goes down and you give up. The match is over. You've been defeated by both your opponent and your brain. Thank you, brain.

This is the worst kind of defeat. No one feels good about losing control of their emotions and giving up. You learn very little from the defeat. There are no positives to take away. Ideally you want to eliminate this type of loss from your game completely. How can you do this?

Change tactics

Let's switch on our tactical mindset again. If you keep losing points in the same way, try something different. It's very frustrating watching a player keep making the same mistakes and then give up halfway through the match without even trying to change tactics. For example, if you keep losing pushing rallies, stop getting involved in pushing rallies. Play positively. Topspin the ball rather than push. When you're serving (which accounts for 50% of points), serve topspin – this will help you avoid getting into pushing rallies in the first place.

Another example – if you're making lots of unforced attacking errors, just keep the ball on the table for a few points. See if your opponent will make mistakes instead of you. In a league match a few years ago, which I still remember very vividly, one of my teammates was playing poorly against a weaker opponent. He kept smashing the ball into the net. His opponent didn't have to do anything to win the points. As they changed ends, I pulled my teammate to one side. I told him to stop smashing, just get the ball on the table and place it in awkward positions. I knew if he did this, his opponent was likely to make a mistake first. What happened in the next game? He won 11-0! A simple change in tactics quickly turned a losing position into a winning one.

Target the weakness

If you're really struggling in a match, try to identify your opponent's weakness and really target it. This will give you a renewed focus and a glimmer of hope, if your opponent struggles to adjust. In a match last season, I was playing some lovely topspin attacks cross-court, but the ball kept coming back quickly, forcing me to miss the next shot. My opponent's forehand block was very good. I was one game behind and struggling. I then realised his backhand block was much weaker. What did I do? I just kept attacking his backhand. Almost every time I did this I won the point. If I had kept attacking his forehand, I'm sure I would have lost the match. By targeting his weakness, I ended up winning quite easily.

In another match last season, I was winning comfortably and playing very well. I was two games up and winning 8-4 in the third. In this situation many players have already given up. Not this opponent. He kept trying different things and eventually worked out that I really struggle with fast sidespin serves to my backhand. What did he do? He kept using this serve and kept winning points. His confidence grew. I became nervous. What should have been a comfortable victory, turned into a close match. I was lucky to eventually win the match 12-10 in the 4th game, but it was a struggle. If my opponent had identified my weakness earlier in the match, I'm sure he would have won.

Go slow between points

When you're not playing well and losing, you may feel like you want to finish the match as quickly as possible. You speed up between points, serve without thinking, make stupid mistakes and then rush on to the next point. Avoid doing this. Instead, go slow between points. This will give you some extra thinking time. Use the time to plan tactics. If it's your serve, spend a moment to think about which serve has been most successful against your opponent. Visualise what shot you want to play if your opponent returns your serve. If it's his serve, take a little longer

10-2, you should still keep trying. Some players switch have a big lead. Some players get tense when they have a her way, there is often an opportunity to win a few points. d be your aim. If you can win two, three or four points at ame in which you're losing heavily, this can really help tum. You still may lose the game, but you'll be more he beginning of the next game and you'll be the player in

y, you will make a miraculous comeback, and what a Your opponent is winning 10-4, but he eases off, thinking on. You win a couple of points. 10-6. Now there's a little your opponent starts to get tense. You win two more Now the pressure on your opponent is unbearable and the him to make silly mistakes. Before you know it, you have e points, win the next two points and win the game 12-10. y not giving up when 10-4 behind.

solutely nothing wrong with losing a game of table tennis. better to lose a match having tried to alter the outcome, st giving up when things aren't going well. Sometimes you pt that an opponent is simply a lot better than you. The inning are unlikely, no matter what you try. Even in these you focus on tactics, exploiting weaknesses and staying ll often be surprised by how many points you do win.

liant feeling when you do turn a match around. You're eat, but you don't give up without a fight. You get advice mate. You change tactics. You start winning points. The hanges, your opponent crumbles, and you win the match. ed because of your positive mindset. Thank you, brain!

getting back to the table. Use th
return the serve and where you
rushing to get on with the next p
the same mistakes. If you go slow
opportunity to identify what isn't
instead.

Ask f

If you're losing and not sure wh
advice. They may be able to spot s
or suggest alternative tactics to try.
advice when matches are going ba
or embarrassed, and just want to b
There's nothing wrong with adm
actively seek advice, rather than re
over. If your body language says "
leave you alone. But if you approa
suggestions, they will be happy to
coaches won't always have the desir
and not sure what to do, what have

Never g

If losing a game heavily, some pla
can concentrate on the next game. Th
and try again. I don't like this approa

if you're losin
off when they
game point. E
And this shou
the end of a
swing mome
confident for
form.

Occasiona
feeling that is.
the game is w
pressure and
points. 10-8.
tension cause
saved six gam
It all started
There's al
But it's much
rather than ju
have to acce
chances of w
situations, if
positive, you
It's a bri
staring at de
from a team
momentum
It all happe

The winning secret

We all like to win. It's a nice feeling. It validates all the time and effort we have committed to pursuing our table tennis goals. Winning gives us a confidence boost. It strokes our ego and makes us feel happy. Yes, winning is nice. But focusing too much on winning - making winning our sole goal - can be counter-productive. It can lower our performance level and restrict our potential to improve. Really, really, really wanting to win can be bad for you.

Here's a personal example. I'm competitive. I grew up with three brothers. We were always competing against each other in everything - toy car races, paper aeroplane races, running races, computer games, music competitions, table tennis, tennis, squash, football. Anything you can think of, we'd find a way of turning it into a competition. This competitiveness has stayed with me always, but when it came to table tennis, I struggled to channel my competitiveness in a productive way. This was my usual pre-match routine:

As match-day approached, I would start to get a little excited.

"Yes, I'm going to win my matches. If I win all three, then my win percentage will increase to 70%."

But then my thoughts would turn to the worst-case scenario.

"What if I lose all three? My win percentage is going to drop. It will be closer to 50%. Hmm, that's not so good. What will others think if I lose these matches?"

To reassure myself, I would then go to the league website and study the win percentages of my opponents.

"Hmm, *Player A* has a 60% win percentage. That's about the same as me. This will be a close match. I'm not sure I'm going to win this one. *Player B* has a 30% win percentage. I should win this one, but what if I lose? That will be a bad defeat. *Player C* has a 90% win percentage. I have no chance against this player. I'm not going to win this match."

In my mind, I am calculating the likelihood of how many matches I will win and lose.

"I'm definitely not going to beat the 90% player. I may not beat the 60% player. I might only win one match out of three. What will this do to my win percentage?"

Now I'm worried and need more information to reassure myself. I would take a deeper look at each opponent's record - looking to see who he has beat and lost to and how close the scores were.

"The 30% player has actually beat a couple of players I have lost to. Hmm...this may be harder than I thought. If he can beat the player I lost to, then he may beat me also. The 60% player recently thrashed a player I struggled to beat. If he can beat this player easily, then he may thrash me too. The 90% player has beaten all the players I lost to. I have no chance."

I'm now digging myself deeper into a pit of despair! I really want to win. I want to see my win percentage improve, but because I want it so much, I can't stop thinking about what happens if I don't win. I'm worried about losing. Really worried.

What did all this worrying achieve? Absolutely nothing! It just made me really nervous. I was so worried about whether I would win or lose, I would end up playing very cautious table tennis, refusing to take any risks, hoping beyond hope that my opponent would make mistakes and I would sneak a victory. Did this work? Rarely. Was I ever happy with my performances? Never.

Then would come the aftermath. First the bad night's sleep. I would toss and turn all night, in between sleep and semi consciousness, replaying the matches in my head. I would feel crushed. Why do I play so bad? How can I lose to that 30% player? He couldn't even hit the ball properly. Why do I even bother with all this training? Once fully awake in the morning, my mood would be low. I would dwell on the poor performance all day and once again question my ability. Maybe I should just quit playing altogether for a while. I'm clearly no good. I wanted to win so much, but I was playing badly far too often. Something had to change.

Focus on the process of playing

Very gradually, I started to shift my focus. Instead of worrying about the result in the hours before a match, I started to focus on the process of playing. I would think about my match tactics - what tactics should I use against player A, B and C? What is my game plan? I would visualise how I was going to serve and receive, how I was going to open up attacks, and how I was going to move my feet. I stopped looking at my opponent's results. No looking at the league website on match-day! It doesn't matter. It's a distraction. I shifted my focus away from the end result and more towards how I wanted to play. I started to re-evaluate my goals. I wanted to judge my performance on whether I played well. Winning or losing was less important. Gradually, week by week, month by month, I thought more and more about the process of playing.

Indeed, this is what we have been doing throughout this book. In the chapters on serving, returning serves, winning points, tactics and playing matches - we haven't concerned ourselves too much with whether we win or lose. We have been more focused on playing to the best of our ability - developing a strong tactical mindset; devising strategies to win points; working out how to apply our strength to an opponent's weakness. This is the process of playing. And when you focus on the process of playing - rather than the outcome - you win more points. If you win more points, you increase your chances of winning more matches. You get the outcome you want - to win - but you get there via a different route. By focusing on the process of playing – and playing well more often as a consequence – you actually win more matches, which leads to a higher win percentage. By not worrying about winning, you actually win more.

You often hear professional athletes, in all sports, talk about focusing on one point at a time or one match at a time. It sounds very dull and clichéd, but they are simply using the same thought process. They are just really zoned in on the process of playing - performing to the best of their ability - and not worrying too much about the outcome. Competitive sport is unpredictable. One player or team will win. One player or team will lose. But you have far less chance of performing well if you are a bag of nerves worrying about whether you will win or lose. Your best chance of winning is if you play as best you can.

I think about it like this - what will make me sleep well at night? It's not necessarily winning or losing. I have won matches, but been unhappy with my performance and slept terribly. I have lost matches, but been happy with how I've played and slept without stirring. What makes me sleep well is if I'm happy with how I performed. Did I play positively?

Did I implement a good game plan? Was my technique decent? Was my footwork good? Did I return serves well? Did I maintain focus throughout the match? Did I play the way I know I can play? If I can answer yes to these questions, I'm happy. And of course, if I can answer yes to all these questions, I have a far higher chance of actually winning. If I play well, which results in a win, then I can definitely sleep well at night!

Reflecting

The match is over. Maybe you won, maybe you lost, but that's not the end of it. Over the coming hours and days you have an opportunity to reflect. How did you perform? Did you serve well? Did your tactics work? Is there anything you would do differently next time?

To help organise my thoughts, I make notes. I have a folder on my computer with notes about many opponents I find difficult to beat. I make notes about an opponent's playing style, how I lost points, how I won points and what tactics to try the next time we play. This has many benefits for me. It helps develop my analytical and tactical thinking, and it helps identify any problem areas which I need to address. For example, when I started writing notes, this issue of returning serves kept coming up. I was leaking points because I struggled to return a variety of different serves. The note-taking made me confront this issue. I started working on returning serves more in my practice sessions, so I could improve this area of my game.

Note-taking also helps me to process defeats. I analyse the match and think through why my opponent won more points than me. I plan some different tactics I can try the next time I play this opponent. I find this provides some psychological relief. It stops me dwelling on a defeat. I have analysed it, identified why I may have lost and I have developed a plan for the next match. Done. Finished. Over. Time to move on.

In my notes, I generally include details about an opponent's playing style, details of what happens when we play, and a few tactics to try for the next match. Each document is probably 250-500 words. When I first moved up to the top division in Cambridge, I lost to the same player twice. This player was not particularly strong – his win percentage was quite low – but I had trouble with his playing style. He was quite steady, with good ball placement and very consistent. Nothing spectacular, but for some reason, I struggled against him. Here are the notes I made after my second defeat:

"Last night Clive beat me quite comfortably. He plays an open topspin game, but he is very steady. He is consistent and defends well with steady blocks. His backhand is spinny and caused me many problems. He kept me off balance with well-placed shots, so I found it hard to attack consistently. He could return most of my serves, and I was not preparing properly for a third ball attack. I would play passively and he would dominate. His own service game is not strong, but I didn't take advantage. I used safe returns which didn't put him under pressure. I didn't play technically or tactically very well.

Tactics for next time…

- His strength is topspin rallies, played at medium speed. I need to avoid playing this type of game with him. I need to either play with more power to win the point quickly or mix in some pushes to change the dynamic of the match.
- Most of his serves are either light topspin or no spin, so there is plenty of opportunity to play faster returns. I should try to be aggressive. I may miss a few but if I can get 50%-60% good returns I'm going to win more points than doing softer returns.

- He is very good at returning most serves. He doesn't return with blistering pace, he just gets them all back. I should just accept he will return my sidespin serves and focus instead on my positioning after my serve to do a good third ball attack.
- His forehand is weaker than his backhand. I should play more to his forehand side and only occasionally switch to his backhand. This should bring my forehand into the game more too.
- Finally, I have to attack with power, otherwise it is too easy for him to return."

My notes are nothing special. I'm not writing an award-winning book. They just need to make sense to me. You can write your notes in any form. You might want to write more detail or keep notes much simpler. It doesn't really matter. You can make notes in whichever form that makes sense to you. It is the process of making notes - developing your analytical and tactical thinking - which matters more than the format of the notes. It forces you to problem-solve - to really think through what happened during a match - and how you may play differently next time.

Revenge!

It may be several months before I face the same opponent again. If I don't make notes, I tend to forget the detail of the previous encounter. There is a danger that I will repeat the same tactical mistakes again. However, if I write notes and prepare tactics, I can quickly remind myself what happened the last time we played.

Let's return to the example above. I lost to the same player twice in one season. After the second loss, I made some notes and came up with some new tactics to try. A few months passed by. Then I faced the opponent again. Before the match, I read my notes. I reminded myself what happened and what tactics I should try. I had written five tactics, but this is a little too many to think about at once. Instead, I focused on one tactic - playing aggressively to his weaker forehand. I wasn't sure if the tactic was going to work, but I had a focus. I had something different to try.

And guess what? It did work. By taking his stronger backhand out of the game, I was getting much easier balls to attack. We were playing far more forehand to forehand rallies, which favoured me as I could attack more aggressively. I won the first two games comfortably. In the third game, I eased off a bit. My attacks were more tame and I played to his backhand more. I lost this game. I had deviated from the tactics I had planned in my notes. As the notes were fresh in my head, I could remind myself again to target the forehand and attack strongly. I did this and won the match. It was my note-taking and tactical thinking which made the difference.

I'm a big fan of making notes on opponents. It doesn't guarantee that I will turn a loss into a victory, but very often my notes help me perform better the next time I play the same opponent. Note-taking is great for developing your analytical and tactical skills, which are extremely helpful when playing matches. A player with good tactical skills, but less technical ability will often beat a player with good technique but poor tactical skills. Your brain can be just as effective as your body in helping you win matches. So use it.

loud 'ding' noise and the ball would shoot up into the air. The floor was a bit of a hazard. Tree roots were exposed, making it hard to move from side to side, without twisting your ankle. The wind was also quite a challenge. Anything between 3 mph and 10 mph was OK, but if the wind speed was above 10 mph, then it became hard to play.

However, it was better than nothing. It was the only opportunity to play some table tennis. I would play twice a week with two other players. I had seen these players at the club, before the lockdown, but I had never played with them. We would have a knock-up and a chat, do a couple of drills and then play lots of matches. The winner would stay on the table. At the beginning of the summer I could beat both players quite easily. In particular, I could dominate with my serve. Both players struggled with my long, fast pendulum serve. They couldn't read when I did sidespin with topspin and when I did sidespin with backspin. I won many cheap points.

As the summer progressed an interesting thing happened. One of the players gradually got much better at returning my serves and the match scores became closer. The other player made no improvement. He still couldn't read the spin and didn't know what shot to play. He would say things like "I hate that serve" or "I just can't return that serve" or "That serve is too good for me". Both players were of a similar standard, but over the period of two months, one player made an impressive improvement and the other player made no improvement at all.

After one session, we all sat on the grass together. I asked the player who had improved how he was able to return my serves. He replied, "I looked online". I was intrigued and wanted to know more. I asked a few more questions, and he gave me an insight into his thought process. After our first match, when he struggled to return any of my pendulum serves, his first instinct was to find out more about the serve. He searched online to find information about the serve - how to do it, what spin was generated and how to return it. He learnt more about reading service spin and how to pick out the difference in motion between sidespin with backspin and sidespin with topspin. He spent some time alone on the outdoor table practising the serve, so he could understand it more.

Every time we played, he tried to apply what he had learnt online. He experimented with different ways of returning my serves. If he made a mistake - no problem. He would quietly work out what he did wrong and then adjust next time. After two months, he was able to return my pendulum serve most of the time. I would still catch him out occasionally, but it was an impressive improvement. Having heard this explanation, the other player - the one who had made no improvement - simply said "I don't think I'll ever be able to return that serve".

In this example one player displayed a strong problem-solving mindset. The other player did not. The non-problem solver was resigned to not being able to return my serves. I was simply the better player. End of story. But the problem solver really wanted to work out how to return my serve. He knew there must be a solution. He just needed to find it. This curiosity - the belief that any problem can be solved - allowed him to improve his game. Over the summer he became a much stronger player.

A problem-solving mindset is a key ingredient for continual improvement. Instead of saying, "I can't do this" or "This is too hard", you should ask yourself "*How* do I do this?". Table tennis is just one enormous puzzle which needs to be solved. How do I attack a backspin ball? How do I block heavy topspin? How do I return a sidespin serve?

How do I switch between backhand and forehand shots efficiently? How do I generate more spin? How do I beat a pusher? How do I control my nerves? How can I beat this player? These are all problems that can be solved if you are curious, open-minded, willing to experiment and persistent. Some problems can be solved quickly. Other problems take years. Strong problem solvers get there in the end.

You can often tell whether a player is a strong problem solver or not by his or her attitude towards long pimples. Many players hate long pimples. They think it is unfair. They do not enjoy playing against long pimples. They don't know how to play against long pimples. They may even give up before the match has started, as they know they will lose. They would prefer long pimples to be banned completely from the sport. Other players take a different approach. They take an interest in how long pimples work. They want to know the effect long pimples have on the ball. They want to know how to respond to the changes in spin. They want to know how to beat a long pimples player.

Which type of player is the problem solver? Which approach is best? These are the two easiest questions I have asked in this book. The former see long pimples as a problem, but are not interested in finding a solution, other than banning them. The latter also see long pimples as a problem, but one which can be overcome. The latter learn how to play against long pimples. They acquire knowledge about how long pimples work. They seek long pimples players to practise against. And guess what? They get good against long pimples. Problem solved.

My topspin problem

A few years ago, when I was playing in Division 2 of the Cambridge league, I faced an opponent who was very good at fast topspin rallies. He played with strong topspin on both his forehand and his backhand. He could switch easily between backhand topspin and forehand topspin. He could play topspin shot after topspin shot. As my team-mate described him - he was a topspin machine! I could keep a random topspin rally going for five or six balls. He could keep a rally going for 20 balls and more. He could always hit one more shot than me in these topspin exchanges. I simply couldn't compete and lost the match heavily.

A few months later we played again, and I tried a different strategy. I knew that if I tried to compete with him in topspin exchanges, I would lose. My plan was to tie him up with backspin. Lots of backspin serves. Lots of pushes. I wanted to frustrate him and turn the game ugly. It didn't work. He still managed to turn enough rallies into topspin exchanges, which of course he won far more often than not. The score was closer this time, but I still lost. This frustrated me. I simply couldn't compete with him in topspin rallies. This was a problem which needed solving. And it was quite a big problem too. I aspired to play in the top division - and do well - but in the top division, there would be more of these very good topspin players.

After that second loss, I made a decision. I had to improve my topspin rallying skills. I spent a long time - two solid years - working on my topspin strokes, my footwork, my ability to switch between backhand and forehand, reading my opponent and my ball placement. I had to improve at this. I wanted to turn it into a strength and start a match knowing I could out-rally my opponent. Did I solve this problem?

Age is no barrier

Table tennis is a sport you can play all your life. You can play competitively if you are 60, 70, 80 or 90-years-old. As we age, we do decline physically. We are not as fast, strong and nimble as we once were. But the great thing about table tennis at the amateur level, is that power and athleticism are not essential to win matches. This gives huge scope for older players to keep improving, regardless of how old they are.

I coach a player in his 80s called Harold. When he was younger Harold was a defensive player, but now he is in his 80s, it's not so easy for him to run around behind the table and keep retrieving balls. It's no longer effective for him, as he doesn't have the physical conditioning to play like this. So, Harold has had to change his playing style, from a defensive chopper to something more attacking, playing closer to the table. This has not been easy. In fact, it's been very difficult. But Harold has made huge progress, and he has succeeded in changing many of his defensive habits.

In our first coaching session in 2015, Harold turned up with an old pimples bat. He liked to push and swipe and chop but didn't have any conventional attacking strokes (drives or topspins). Because of his age, I didn't want to change too much. I thought it was too late in his life to make significant changes to technique. My approach was to take his existing playing style and technique and improve it where possible.

But Harold wasn't satisfied with this. His existing defensive playing style was becoming less effective because he didn't have the speed and agility to keep retrieving balls. He wanted to change. He wanted to ditch his pimples bat. He wanted to learn how to drive and topspin. He wanted a playing style where he could win points quicker and didn't need to move around as much. He wanted to change from a defensive player to an attacking player. I knew this would be a challenge, bearing in mind that Harold was 80. I have numerous habits I have tried to change over the years, and I know how hard it can be, and how long it can take. But Harold was determined to change, so we went with it.

Fixing the forehand

The toughest challenge we faced was changing Harold's forehand technique. When he was younger Harold would always chop with his forehand. He developed a strong habit of always doing a backswing where the bat went up, with the bat face open. He must have played this stroke thousands and thousands of times. The habit was very ingrained. The pathways in his brain were very deep. His muscle memory was very established.

This backswing is great for chopping but makes life difficult if trying to drive or topspin, where the backswing needs to be lower and the bat angle more closed. We spent session after session, trying to change the backswing and bat angle. It could take all session just to get a basic forehand drive working. Progress! But in the next session the backswing would revert to his old chopping style. We would repeat everything we'd previously done and get the forehand drive working again. Progress! Then next session, back to the chopping style again.

Sometimes Harold would get the backswing right, but the bat angle would be all wrong and the ball would keep going off the end of the table. Other times the bat angle would be right, but the backswing would be too high, and he would hit down on the ball and put it into the net. At times, we both despaired, and we had very honest conversations about whether we should continue trying to develop his drives and topspins. It just seemed so hard to change Harold's habits.

Perseverance

One of the remarkable things about Harold is how determined he is to improve at his age. He didn't want to give up. Even though it was very difficult for him to change, he embraced the challenge. He wanted to learn and master new techniques, so we kept going.

As the months and years passed, his forehand drive slowly began to improve. Each session it would take less time to get his forehand drive technique working. His chopping backswing was gradually disappearing. New pathways in Harold's brain were being formed. Eventually, Harold was able to start a session playing forehand drives with no instruction from me whatsoever. His backswing was in the right place. His bat angle was correct. He could hit 10, 20, 30 forehand drives with no errors. Despite being in his 80s, and despite having a lifetime of playing his forehand in a certain way, he was able to change. He was able to transform his forehand from a defensive stroke into an attacking stroke. He would turn up to a coaching session with a big grin on his face and tell me about how he used his forehand drive to beat one of his friends. Not only had Harold learnt new technique, he was actually using it successfully in a match.

If Harold can change some heavily ingrained habits in his 80s, then surely anyone can change. Harold knew he couldn't play his old defensive style effectively any more because he wasn't agile enough. If he wanted to keep playing, and being competitive with his peers, he had to change the way he played. Harold completely embraced this massive challenge. He knew it would take a lot of work, but he was open-minded and willing to try new things.

Harold came to me to get help and advice. This accelerated the learning process. I could quickly see if there was anything obvious he wasn't doing correctly and help him fix it. I showed him how to do a forehand drive and gave him drills to practise the shot. Even though I gave Harold some help, none of his improvement would have happened without all the hard work he put in himself. Harold did a lot of practice with his robot at home and during practice sessions. Practice, practice, practice, practice, practice. More practice. Even when he was starting to get it right, he went away to do even more practice. He kept repeating the same action again and again (thousands of times) to establish new muscle memory. It was very tough and it took a long time, but he did it.

If you want to change a table tennis habit, you really need to commit to it. You can't approach the task half-heartedly. Embrace the challenge, get some help and just keep persevering. It can take a long, long time to change a habit – to change your muscle memory – but it can be done. I have done it with my own game. Harold has done it in his 80s. Age really is no barrier to improvement.

Overcoming adversity

It's March 2015 and it's the last match of the season. My final opponent is an older female player – slim, tall, silver haired, with a determined spring in her step. I am expected to win, but I feel a little uneasy. I'm not quite sure how to approach the match. Part of me feels like I should take it easy. I don't want to be seen trying too hard against an older female opponent. But another part of me knows if I don't try my best I may end up losing.

The match begins. My opponent defends well with her long pimples. In fact, she defends very well. My big topspin shots keep coming back. If I misjudge the spin from her pimples, the ball pops up high, and she drives the ball hard with her forehand for a winner.

The score is close. This causes me to tense up and I make a couple of mistakes. At 8-8, I compose myself, and two good serves and third ball attacks brings up game point. Then an untypical service error from my opponent and I win the first game 11-8. Phew!

~

My opponent is Margaret Chambers, aged 64, from St George's Table Tennis club in Cambridge. On the table she is very focused, showing little emotion, but clearly determined to win. Off the table Margaret is warm and talkative. After the match, I get to know more about

Margaret's background – an inspiring tale of late sporting success and triumph over adversity following a horrific car accident.

Margaret started playing table tennis when she was 13. If the courts weren't playable at her local tennis club, Margaret and her twin sister Anne, would go to the clubhouse and play table tennis instead. Her interest in table tennis grew, and with Anne, she played in local leagues in Bedford and Southport. Then college beckoned and table tennis stopped, for nearly 40 years. But Margaret continued to play a number of different sports. She was captain of the GB colleges netball team, played tennis at county level and badminton at recreational level.

However, Margaret's main sporting success was still to come. At the age of 30, she started to play squash and was soon playing at county level. In 2003, at the age of 53, she was selected to represent England in the over 50s category in home internationals played in Antrim, Northern Ireland. Margaret remained undefeated throughout the tournament and England were crowned champions.

On the experience of representing her country Margaret said, "I was so thrilled to get the call-up letter. My brother and sister-in-law, who live in Dublin, came and supported. It was extra special for me as my teammates had played before at this level and most of them in other age categories as well. It was a once in a life-time experience."

~

In the second game of our match, I begin to relax a little more and build up a healthy lead. But then Margaret ups her level. Her chops come back low over the net, loaded with backspin. A forehand topspin goes into the net. In the next point I misread the spin and my forehand topspin goes off the end of the table. And then another error resulting from Margaret's uncompromising defensive strokes.

All of a sudden the score is 8-8 again. With enthusiastic support from her sister Anne, I'm feeling the pressure once more. I change tactics and play a bit more cautiously, hoping Margaret will make an error. I misread the spin (again). The ball pops up, but this time Margaret misses an easy attack. Lucky! Another tense rally goes my way. And with a side spin serve to Margaret's elbow and a big forehand attack I win the game 11-8. This is hard work.

~

In November 2003 – the same year as her call up to the England squash team – Margaret was involved in a serious car crash. She suffered multiple injuries including imploded fractures to her forehead, fractures to her ulna and radius in her right arm, a fractured kneecap, multiple fractures to bones in her right hand, damage to her rotator cuff and multiple abrasions around her eyes, neck and legs.

Margaret could not work for six months. It was over a year before she returned to playing squash competitively. When she started playing squash again she had to use a two handed grip because she couldn't manage with one hand. Margaret could never recapture the form which led her to represent England. The injuries sustained in the car crash had taken their toll. The unforgiving physicality of squash seemed incompatible with an ageing and creaking body. It became very apparent to Margaret that she could not play to the same standard as before the car crash.

But Margaret is a very determined competitor. Not playing sport wasn't an option. So, she returned to the sport she first played as a 13-year-old – table tennis. Along with her sister Anne, she started playing at St George's table tennis club in Cambridge. Encouraged by club coach Kevin Gray, Margaret was soon practising regularly, sometimes as much as four times a week. Before long she was playing in two local leagues, and her win percentage was getting higher and higher.

I was due to play Margaret earlier in the season, but she was unable to play. The reason? She was having a hip replacement. I never expected her to play in the second half of the season. But six weeks after the operation she was practising again. Eight weeks after the operation she was playing league matches again. The hip operation aided her movement. She told me "I usually feel more secure and have little pain-discomfort. But you cannot 100% replace a hip with a new one. But at 64, who has a 100% body? You do what you can with what you have. You do your best."

~

In the third game of our match, I'm in trouble. Margaret is winning 7-4 and her defence is more consistent than my attack. In one ridiculous rally, I hit four topspin shots, moving Margaret around the table, but the ball keeps coming back. My fifth topspin lands deep to Margaret's backhand. Slightly out of position, Margaret switches her bat from her right hand to her left hand and blocks the ball back over the net. The ball clips the edge of the table and Margaret wins the point. The few spectators applaud. And I can't help but smile. I glance at my teammate

Yordan, who is umpiring, and he gives me a raised eyebrow. He doesn't look impressed.

To get back into the game I know I have to play my very best. I add more power to my attacks and start to find a way through Margaret's defence. The score is 14-13 and I have match-point. Another sidespin serve to Margaret's elbow and a big forehand attack down the line and I've won. I am very, very relieved.

~

This match took place five years before the publication of this book. Since the match Margaret has continued to confuse and frustrate opponents with her defensive skills. She has moved up divisions and is still winning many matches. She continues to improve.

Certainly, her participation in other sports helps her compete. She believes table tennis shares many of the same fundamentals with other racquet sports, such as preparation, watching the ball, shot selection, movement, decision-making, psychological and physical stamina. And by her own admission she has many strengths, honed over many years of competitive play, which she brings to the table. "I'm usually strong mentally and don't make too many unforced errors. My analysis of opponents and endurance is relatively good. My concentration and focus is quite strong and I'm competitive."

Even though Margaret is fiercely competitive, it's not the winning which she really cares about. I sense a deep desire within her to always develop her skills - to continually improve. Part of her evolution has been the addition of attacking strokes to her existing defensive repertoire. She has consulted other players and coaches - including me -

to help her with her drives and topspins. She really wants to develop this area of her game, as it will help her compete with and beat stronger players. Her eagerness to learn is contagious.

I really admire Margaret's can-do attitude. It's very easy to lower our expectations when we suffer a setback, especially if we experience a physical injury. We can hide behind it as an excuse as to why we are not playing well or improving. However, Margaret's story shows that whatever life throws at you – injuries, accidents, general wear and tear – there are new activities you can do, new sports you can play, new ways to enjoy life. And most importantly, whatever activity you choose to do, you can keep on improving.

Margaret is keen to stress she doesn't think her situation is remarkable. "There are lots of players out there with replacement joints. And lots of older players dealing with all sorts, not to mention younger ones too." But I think she is selling herself short. Her game requires a lot of side to side and back and forth movement. To do this in her sixties, having recovered from such a serious car crash, is very impressive indeed. If I can still move and play like Margaret when I'm in my sixties and if I still have Margaret's appetite to learn, improve and compete, I'll be very happy indeed.

No matter how good you get, there's always someone better

You work hard in training. Your level improves. You beat more and more players. You feel confident about your table tennis skills. Then you face a higher level player who identifies and exploits every weakness in your game and wins the match easily. It's a humbling experience and makes you doubt your ability to play table tennis. It's a reminder that no matter how good you think you're getting at table tennis, there's always better players who can make you feel like a beginner.

You can take these defeats in one of two ways. You can get down on yourself, tell yourself you'll never be as good as others at table tennis, and lose motivation to play. Over the years I have seen several players move up a division, suffer heavy losses, get despondent and eventually stop playing. They just didn't think they were good enough to play at a higher level, so gave up.

This is one approach, but as you can imagine, it's not an approach I recommend! A better approach is to embrace the challenge. When you move up a level and face better players, just accept that you're going to have some heavy defeats. This is OK. It's normal. It's just a part of any competitive sport.

No matter how good you get, there is always a better player. If I were to play someone ranked in the top 50 of England, I will probably lose by a comfortable margin. But a player ranked 50 in England is likely to get beaten easily by a player ranked top in the top five in England. A professional player ranked 100 in the world is likely to get easily beaten by a player ranked top 10 in the world. Imagine how that feels? You're a professional player, training 20-30 hours per week, and by most people's standards, pretty amazing at table tennis. But you play someone ranked in the top 10 in the world, get a good beating, and feel quite inadequate. So, we all face this situation, even professional players. There is always a better player, capable of making you look silly (unless you happen to be the number one player in the world).

What really matters is how you respond to the challenge of playing better players. If you accept that there will always be a higher standard - a better player - then losses don't become a crushing blow to your ego, just an opportunity to learn. You can use these defeats to learn about your weaknesses. Did you keep pushing the ball into the net? Did you keep missing the table with your attacks? Did you lose points straight from your opponent's serve? Did you give your opponent easy balls to attack? If you don't find it easy to analyse your performance, ask for feedback from someone else who watched the match – a coach or another player - or even your opponent. They will spot things about your game you may not even be aware of.

You can also use these defeats to learn about a stronger player's strengths. What can this player do, which you can't? What tactics does she use? How does she play her shots? What is her playing style? There is so much to learn from playing a stronger player. This can influence what you do in training and how you develop your playing style and tactics in the future. It shows you the path to playing at a higher level.

It can take a lot of effort and deliberate practice to move up a level at table tennis. The higher you play, the more effort is required to reach the next level. Significant improvement doesn't always happen quickly. It will take time. If you get thrashed by a stronger player, it's unlikely you will win the next time you play. But you shouldn't worry about that too much. No one is expecting you to win. Your goal is simply to be more competitive - to win more points and to raise your level. This will give you a lot of encouragement for the future. You may not win the next few times you play either, but if you can get the scoreline closer each time, you know you're going in the right direction. Over time, you can catch-up and eventually beat a player who once seemed so much better than you.

One day, I'd like to be veteran world champion. How cool would that be? Realistically, it's never going to happen, unless I live to 100-years-old and all the better players die before I do! To reach such a high standard, I will need to improve my game massively. I will need to compete with - and beat - players who are currently a lot better than me. This goal is wildly difficult - many would say completely unrealistic - and I would agree. But by willing to take on players who are stronger than me - and learning from the defeats in a positive way - I will continue to improve. I may never reach the top of amateur table tennis, but in the process of trying to reach the top, I will get much better at table tennis than I ever imagined. So join me on this journey. Maybe we'll play against each other in a veteran tournament somewhere in the world. You should have an advantage, as you now know all my table tennis secrets! See you at the table.

Follow your own path

Thank you for reading my book. If you have made it this far you deserve a medal - a table tennis medal, of course!

I have shared a lot of tips and advice in this book. Hopefully some of my tips will work for you and help you win some extra points, beat that player you have never beaten before, and generally elevate your game to a higher level. But it's quite possible that some of my tips won't work for you. Maybe they seem a little alien and don't quite fit with your playing style. If that's the case, then please ignore. The tips I have shared in this book are biased towards my own experience, playing style, and strengths and weaknesses. Your playing style may be completely different. If a particular piece of advice doesn't work, try a different approach which makes more sense to you.

And this is the key message I want to leave you with. In amateur table tennis, there are so many different ways to play and succeed. There is not one single 'correct' path. You don't have to play like a Chinese professional to win matches in local league and amateur tournaments. You can play however you want. You could be a push-blocker, a topspin attacker, a long pimples chopper or just a general mix of everything. Any playing style can work in amateur table tennis. Your technique doesn't have to be amazing - just consistent and effective. There are endless tactical options available for every playing style. You just need to discover and master the tactics which work best for you.

On your table tennis journey you will encounter many different viewpoints. You will get tips from other players and coaches. You will watch YouTube videos. You will read articles and books. There is a wealth of information available on how to win at table tennis. Embrace this. Read, watch, ask questions and consult. Keep an open mind, but remember that not all advice will benefit you. Every player, coach and online expert has a different approach and a different way of playing. Adopt the advice which benefits your game. Discard the advice which doesn't help. Nobody has a monopoly on table tennis wisdom. There are just a lot of different perspectives. Follow your own path.

If you train regularly, develop consistent technique and work on your match-play skills you will progress a lot more than you imagine. But as you strive to improve, increase your win percentage, move up a division or win a local tournament, don't forget to enjoy yourself. Table tennis should be fun. This is why we all started playing in the first place. It's just really enjoyable hitting a small ball, over a small net, with a small bat. Never lose sight of this. Appreciate your opponents, learn from your defeats and revel in your victories.

Fancy a game?

Acknowledgments

I have always wanted to publish a book. I'm sure the 23-year-old Tom would have anticipated some world changing political masterpiece. But life takes us in unexpected directions, and a career obsessing about table tennis is certainly a more unusual turn of events. But now that my life is full of the joys of balls pinging and ponging, I wouldn't want it any of other way.

I must give thanks to Sanket Shah, for being so welcoming and encouraging when I first turned up at Finsbury Table Tennis Club in London. He helped nurture my table tennis addiction and showed me it was possible to earn a living from the sport.

Most of the ideas I have presented in this book are not original. I have been influenced by many other coaches and players including Mark Mitchell, Larry Hodges, Ferenc Horvath, Craig Bryant, Alois and Jeff from Ping Skills and many others. I thank you all for my development both as a player and as a coach.

My teammates - James Ward, Yordan Zaykov, Daniel Hearne-Potton, Dan Smally and Ferenc Horvath - are a great source of encouragement during league matches. They constantly remind me to stop playing like a coach and start attacking. I have learnt a lot watching you all play, and this has helped shape many of the ideas in this book.

A special thank you to Martin Gray, for continuing to practice with me, despite beating me every time we play. These beatings highlight all my weaknesses, but shine a light on my path to improvement. You have helped shape my thinking about technique, playing styles and unorthodox shots.

Thanks to all the players I coach. I am continually amazed by how much improvement is possible when a player approaches table tennis with a curious mind and a lot of purposeful practice. Every coaching session I learn something new, much of which is reflected in this book.

Thank you to David Howard and Jodi Manning for giving up so much time to proof-read. Hopefully between us we have spotted most of my typos!

And finally, a big thank you to my Mum and Dad for introducing me to table tennis and the special holiday memories, and to Jodi, Franz, Beatrix and Oliver for supporting my obsession. Love to you all.